FAITH-BASED
ORGANIZATIONS:
CURRENT ISSUES

FAITH-BASED ORGANIZATIONS: CURRENT ISSUES

BEN CANADA AND DAVID M. ACKERMAN

Novinka Books
New York

Senior Editors: Susan Boriotti and Donna Dennis
Coordinating Editor: Tatiana Shohov
Office Manager: Annette Hellinger
Graphics: Wanda Serrano
Editorial Production: Marius Andronie, Maya Columbus, Vladimir Klestov,
   Matthew Kozlowski and Tom Moceri
Circulation: Ave Maria Gonzalez, Vera Popovic, Raymond Davis,
   Melissa Diaz, Magdalena Nuñez, Marlene Nuñez and Jeannie Pappas
Communications and Acquisitions: Serge P. Shohov

Library of Congress Cataloging-in-Publication Data
Available Upon Request

ISBN: 1-59033-708-5.

Copyright © 2003 by Novinka Books, An Imprint of
   Nova Science Publishers, Inc.
   400 Oser Ave, Suite 1600
   Hauppauge, New York 11788-3619
   Tele. 631-231-7269   Fax 631-231-8175
   e-mail: Novascience@earthlink.net
   Web Site: http://www.novapublishers.com

All rights reserved. No part of this book may be reproduced, stored in a retrieval system or transmitted in any form or by any means: electronic, electrostatic, magnetic, tape, mechanical photocopying, recording or otherwise without permission from the publishers.

The authors and publisher have taken care in preparation of this book, but make no expressed or implied warranty of any kind and assume no responsibility for any errors or omissions. No liability is assumed for incidental or consequential damages in connection with or arising out of information contained in this book.

This publication is designed to provide accurate and authoritative information with regard to the subject matter covered herein. It is sold with the clear understanding that the publisher is not engaged in rendering legal or any other professional services. If legal or any other expert assistance is required, the services of a competent person should be sought. FROM A DECLARATION OF PARTICIPANTS JOINTLY ADOPTED BY A COMMITTEE OF THE AMERICAN BAR ASSOCIATION AND A COMMITTEE OF PUBLISHERS.

Printed in the United States of America

CONTENTS

Preface vii

Chapter 1 Faith-Based Organizations and their Relationship with State and Local Governments: An Analysis of the Potential Impact of Current Legislation 1
Ben Canada

Chapter 2 Public Aid to Faith-Based Organizations in the 107th Congress (Charitable Choice): Background and Selected Legal Issues 33
David M. Ackerman

Index 97

PREFACE

Although enacted into law in four previous statutes, charitable choice has been the subject of persistent controversy; and President Bush's initiative in the 107th Congress led the controversy to become highly visible. The primary concerns have been the constitutionality and desirability of the federal government directly subsidizing faith-based social service programs and whether subsidized religious organizations should be able to discriminate on religious grounds in their employment practices. This new book provides background and analysis on a number of the salient factual and legal issues about charitable choice, and also discusses the relationship of faith-based organizations with state and local governments.

Chapter 1

FAITH-BASED ORGANIZATIONS AND THEIR RELATIONSHIP WITH STATE AND LOCAL GOVERNMENTS: AN ANALYSIS OF THE POTENTIAL IMPACT OF CURRENT LEGISLATION

Ben Canada

SUMMARY

Federal, state, and local governments have long collaborated with faith-based organizations (FBOs) to provide services to needy citizens. The issue of government funding for FBOs (charitable choice) is controversial and is receiving renewed public attention for two main reasons. First, President George W. Bush made a faith-based initiative a priority of his domestic agenda. His Administration hopes to expand tax incentives for private donations to charities, and to eliminate statutory, regulatory, and administrative barriers perceived to prevent FBOs from receiving federal funds. In December 2002, the President issued Executive Order 13279, instructing selected federal agencies to develop charitable choice policies. The second reason for renewed public attention is the 107th Congress's consideration of H.R. 7, and specifically Title II, the "Charitable Choice Act of 2001." Charitable choice rules are intended to allow religious organizations to provide federally funded services from designated programs on the same basis as any other nongovernmental provider, without impairing the religious character of the FBOs or the religious freedom of beneficiaries. Title II proposed expanding provisions of charitable choice law to nine new program areas. H.R. 7 passed the House on July 19, 2001.

A Senate bill, the "Charity Aid, Recovery, and Empowerment Act of 2002" (CARE bill), S. 1924, did not contain extensive charitable choice provisions like those found in Title II in H.R. 7. It did, however, seek to prevent potential discrimination against FBOs in the awarding of federal grants.

State initiatives for increasing FBO access to government funds vary considerably. A limited number of states have enacted legislative and regulatory changes to increase such access and educated state and local officials about charitable choice rules. Others have concentrated their efforts on collaboration and awareness campaigns, rather than legislative or regulatory changes. On the other hand, many states have done little in response to charitable choice law. As with the state experience, local efforts to better utilize FBO resources have also varied.

Supporters of the faith-based initiative offered anecdotal information that FBOs can effectively deliver federally funded services in a wide range of program areas. This initiative, however, raises institutional issues about potential FBO effectiveness, accountability, and the working relationship of FBOs and state and local governments. Effectiveness issues include: range of services; lack of evaluative data; qualifications of FBO personnel; inclusion of religious content; and availability of secular alternatives. Accountability issues include: FBO ability to report results; vouchers and accountability; and separation of government funds. To an extent, questions about FBOs' working relationship with state and local governments are based on some adverse impacts of past efforts to incorporate community-based organizations into federally funded services. Some officials are concerned that new charitable choice legislation could disrupt good working relationships between FBOs and state and local governments. This report will be updated as circumstances warrant.

INTRODUCTION

Federal, state, and local governments have long collaborated with faith-based organizations (FBOs) to provide services to needy citizens. FBOs can include a range of organizational types, but they generally fall into three categories: church congregations, national networks, and nonprofit religious organizations.[1] Some FBOs receive a significant amount of federal funding. In FY2001, for example, Catholic Relief Services received $88 million in federal funds,[2] and World Vision Inc. received $124 million.[3] Most FBOs provide traditional social services, such as homeless programs and substance abuse programs, while others administer economic and community development programs.

Congress enacted the first charitable choice provision in the 1996 welfare reform law, authorizing states to "... administer and provide services under [certain federal] programs ... through contracts with charitable, religious, or private organizations."[4] Charitable choice rules are intended to allow religious organizations[5] to provide federally funded services from designated programs on the same basis as any other nongovernmental provider without impairing the religious character of the organizations or the religious freedom of beneficiaries.

The issue of government funding for FBOs has received renewed public attention for two main reasons. First, President George W. Bush has made a faith-based initiative a priority of his domestic agenda. In January 2001, the President issued a blueprint for his initiative, *Rallying the Armies of Compassion*.[6] In the report, the Administration discussed the components of its faith-based initiative, including expanding tax incentives for private donations to charities, and eliminating statutory, regulatory, and administrative barriers that prevent FBOs from receiving federal funds. The President further established an Office of Faith-Based and Community Initiatives in the White House to coordinate the initiative.[7] The Administration also instructed the Departments of Education, Justice, Labor,

---

[1] John McCarthy and Jim Castelli, *Religion-Sponsored Social Services: The Not-So-Independent Sector*, Nonprofit Sector Research Fund (NSRF), The Aspen Institute, 1999, pp. 53-54. See NSRF web site: [http://www.nonprofitresearch.org/], visited Dec. 18, 2002.

[2] Catholic Relief Services, 2001 Financial Summary, see web site at: [http://www.catholicrelief.org/about_us/financial_information/summary.cfm],visited Dec.18, 2002.

[3] World Vision Inc., 2001 Audited Financial Statement, see web site at: [http://www.worldvision.org/worldvision/comms.nsf/2001ar_home], visited Dec. 18, 2002.

[4] P.L. 104-193, sec. 104(a)(1); 110 stat. 2161. The 1996 welfare law applied charitable choice rules to program areas under Temporary Assistance to Needy Families (TANF), food stamps, Medicaid, Supplemental Security Income, and child support enforcement.

[5] Charitable choice legislation uses the term "religious organization." This report, however, uses the term "faith-based organization" (FBO), a more commonly used term.

[6] U.S. President (George W. Bush), *Rallying the Armies of Compassion*, Jan. 21, 2001. See White House web site: [http://www.whitehouse.gov/news/reports/faithbased.html], visited Dec. 18,2002.

[7] The Office's web site is: [http://www.whitehouse.gov/government/fbci/].

Health and Human Services, and Housing and Urban Development to establish faith-based offices. These departmental offices have sought to increase FBO access to federal grants by reducing regulatory, contractual, and other potential administrative obstacles.[8]

The second reason for renewed public attention is the 107th Congress's consideration of legislation with faith-based components. The most assertive proposal was in H.R. 7 (sponsored by Representatives Hall and Watts), and specifically Title II, the "Charitable Choice Act of 2001." The bill would have expanded FBO access to federal funds in nine program areas addressing crime prevention, juvenile delinquency, substance abuse, housing, job training, elderly services, child abuse, and hunger. It also contained a number of protections for FBOs, as well as for recipients of government-funded services. H.R. 7 passed the House on July 19, 2001.[9]

Faith-based legislation was also introduced in the Senate by Senators Lieberman and Santorum. The Charity Aid, Recovery, and Empowerment Act of 2002 (CARE bill), S. 1924, omitted some of the more contentious charitable choice elements in the House bill. As introduced, it contained tax incentives for charitable giving and provisions addressing equal treatment of all nongovernmental service providers, including FBOs.[10] Unlike Title II of H.R. 7, the CARE bill did not seek to expand FBO access in specific federal programs. The equal treatment provisions were subsequently dropped from the Senate bill. In September 2002, however, the Senate Finance Committee filed a "consensus" manager's amendment (S.Amdt. 4719 to H.R. 5005) that restored the equal treatment provisions.[11] Although H.R. 5005, the "Homeland Security Act" was enacted, the Amendment did not pass. (All references to the CARE bill in this report refer to S.Amdt. 4719, unless otherwise noted.)

Title II of H.R. 7, as well as the proposed CARE bill, raised issues about the relationship between FBOs and state and local governments whose agencies administer federally assisted services. Many state and local officials view the faith-based initiative as an opportunity to enhance services to needy citizens. On the other hand, other public officials have concerns about potential FBO effectiveness, accountability, and their working relationship with FBOs.

---

[8] U.S. President (George W. Bush), "Agency Responsibilities With Respect to Faith-Based and Community Initiatives," Executive Order 13198, *Federal Register*, vol. 66, p. 8497, Jan. 31, 2001.
[9] For an overview of the charitable choice provisions in H.R. 7, see CRS Report RS20948, *Charitable Choice Provisions in H.R. 7*, by Vee Burke.
[10] S. 1924 (as introduced), Title III.
[11] S.Amdt. 4719 to H.R. 5005, Title VII.

In December 2002, the Administration, citing the lack of legislation addressing its faith-based proposals, issued Executive Order 13279 instructing agencies to develop policies that ensure equal treatment and protection for faith-based and community organizations. The order seeks to increase FBO access to federal funds in programmatic areas similar to those addressed in H.R. 7 and the CARE Act, such as children's services, job training, counseling and mentoring, literacy, housing, and substance abuse.[12] A subsequent order also established two additional faith-based offices in the Department of Agriculture and the U.S. Agency for International Development.

Overview of State and Local Faith-Based Initiatives

State and local governments, in general, have a long tradition of collaborating with FBOs to provide services. Since the 1996 charitable choice provisions were enacted, state and local initiatives for increasing FBO-delivered services have varied greatly.

State-level Initiatives

Some states have actively sought to use available FBO resources. These states have undertaken faith-based initiatives by making legislative and regulatory changes to promote FBO access to government funds. Other states have concentrated their efforts on collaboration and awareness campaigns, rather than legislative or regulatory changes. On the other hand, a significant number of states have not acted on existing charitable choice provisions for expanding FBO access to government funds.

By 2000, a few states, such as Arizona, Indiana, Ohio, Texas, Virginia, and Wisconsin, had passed legislation or changed regulations as part of a faith-based initiative.[13] Indiana has actively worked to incorporate FBOs in service delivery. In late 1999, Governor Frank O'Bannon initiated the "FaithWorks Indiana" program in the state Family and Social Services Administration, designed to promote outreach to the faith community. The primary form of assistance consists of workshops and consultations for FBOs in such areas as understanding charitable choice provisions, improving service delivery, grant writing, and financial management. FaithWorks also

---

[12] U.S. President (George W. Bush), "Equal Protection of the Laws for Faith-based and Community Organizations," Executive Order 13279, *Federal Register*, vol. 67, p. 77141, Dec. 16, 2002.

operates a toll-free number and web site that answers questions from FBO personnel. The initiative has provided some form of assistance to hundreds of FBOs in Indiana and is attempting to develop ongoing partnerships in all of the state's 92 counties. Since its creation, the program reports that the state has awarded roughly $4.5 million in contracts to FBOs.[14]

Some states have sought to increase FBO access to government funds through awareness campaigns and collaboration, rather than legislative or regulatory changes. At least 15 states have appointed liaisons to the faith community to promote greater communication and collaboration among government agencies, FBOs, and other community-based organizations.[15] Most of these states have appointed liaisons within state departments administering social services or workforce development programs. Oklahoma and New Jersey have created special offices for faith-based initiatives to promote greater awareness of funding opportunities, and to serve as a single-point-of-contact for FBOs to communicate their views to the state.[16] Some states have appointed local faith liaisons to supplement state-level outreach efforts. For example, Virginia has appointed faith-based contacts in each local social services agency and Texas has appointed regional faith-based liaisons, each of which serves several counties.[17]

These liaisons and other state officials carry out a variety of activities to facilitate government cooperation with FBOs, including:

- workshops on program development, availability of government funds, charitable choice provisions;
- technical assistance with grant administration;
- help with compliance with federal and state regulations;
- identification of best practices and model programs;
- identification of service gaps; and,
- advocacy on behalf of FBOs to state officials and legislators.

---

[13] Center for Public Justice, "Charitable Choice Compliance: A National Report Card," Sept. 2000, [http://www.in.gov/fssa/faithworks/PDFs/Report_6_02.PDF], visited Dec. 18, 2002.

[14] FaithWorks Indiana, Report on first two years activities, 2002. Available at: [http://www.IN.gov/fssa/faithworks/index.html], visited Dec. 18, 2002.

[15] States with official faith liaisons include, but are not limited to: Arizona, Arkansas, California, Colorado, Georgia, Indiana, Maryland, New Jersey, New York, North Carolina, Ohio, Oklahoma, Pennsylvania, Texas, and Virginia.

[16] See Oklahoma State Office of the Faith-Based Liaison web site: [http://www.oklaosf.state.ok.us/~faithlinks/], visited Dec. 18, 2002; and New Jersey Office of Faith-Based Initiatives web site: [http://www.state.nj.us/dca/dhcr/faith.htm], visited Dec. 18, 2002.

[17] Telephone conversations with selected state and local officials, June-July 2001.

In 2000, the Center for Public Justice, a self-described Christian research and advocacy group, rated each state on its efforts to exercise charitable choice provisions in existing legislation. The center gave all but 12 states a "F" rating because it felt they had not passed legislation or changed regulations to fully implement existing charitable choice provisions.[18] On the other hand, some research suggests that states are generally increasing their outreach to FBOs and incorporating them in service delivery.[19]

Local-level Initiatives

Although the role of FBOs in service delivery has only recently received public attention, local governments have long collaborated with FBOs to serve needy citizens. At the local level, just as at the state level, implementation of existing charitable choice provisions has varied. Localities that have sought to employ FBOs in service delivery have done so in a variety of ways, including formal faith-based initiatives, awareness campaigns, and appointment of liaisons.

Proponents of the increased use of FBOs frequently point to Philadelphia as an example of a city that has successfully collaborated with the faith community. Some suggest that Philadelphia has used the resources of FBOs in a greater quantity and variety of services than any other American city.[20] Since taking office in January 2000, Mayor John F. Street has made his faith-based initiative a core component of his plan to improve city services. The mayor and his administration view FBOs as potentially effective partners for delivering specific services, including literacy programs, faith counseling for prison inmates, and counseling for children of inmates, among other things. Mayor Street also hopes to employ FBOs in an effort to reduce the level of truancy in city schools. He has asked FBOs to "adopt" a Philadelphia school and contact the families of truant students. The mayor's initiative has come mostly through collaboration with FBOs, rather than through public funding of their efforts. Reportedly, most of Philadelphia's FBOs receive funding from such charitable foundations as The Pew Charitable Trusts.[21]

---

[18] Center for Public Justice, "Charitable Choice Compliance: A National Report Card."
[19] John C. Green and Amy L. Sherman, *Fruitful Collaborations: A Survey of Government-Funded Faith-Based Programs in 15 States* (Charlottesville, VA: Hudson Institute, Sept. 2002).
[20] Andrea Billups, "Keeping the Faith, Philadelphia's Mayor Helps Make a Difference," *Washington Times*, Apr. 15, 2001, p. A1.
[21] Ibid.

While most local governments may not have been as active as Philadelphia in collaborating with FBOs, a number of localities has designated liaisons to the faith community. According to a 2001 survey sponsored by the U.S. Conference of Mayors, at least 121 mayors had appointed liaisons to the faith community, and 37 more were planning to appoint liaisons.[22] These liaisons are typically charged with facilitating communication between the local government and FBOs, advertising the availability of government grants, and assisting FBOs with grant administration.

ANALYSIS OF SELECTED INSTITUTIONAL ISSUES

Many state and local officials view the faith-based initiative as an opportunity to enhance services. Other officials express have concerns about potential FBO effectiveness and accountability, and the working relationship between state and local governments and FBOs. The remainder of this report discusses institutional issues in the relationship between FBOs and state and local governments. It analyzes issues raised in Title II of H.R. 7, the CARE bill, and E.O. 13279, and explores options that might be considered to address them.

Effectiveness of FBOs

Proponents of using FBOs and other nonprofit groups to deliver services to needy citizens believe these organizations can effectively partner with state and local governments. They argue FBOs are able to effectively utilize the resources of their members and the community, and have greater flexibility over program design than government agencies.

Anecdotal Accounts of Successful Partnerships

Proponents of FBOs have offered much anecdotal evidence about the effectiveness of FBO-delivered programs. A highly publicized example of an effective partnership between a city and its faith community is the Indianapolis Front Porch Alliance, begun in early 1998 by then-Mayor Stephen Goldsmith. Public officials, private citizens, and leaders of FBOs and other community-based organizations serve on the alliance board. Its

---

[22] Laurie Goodstein, "States Steer Religious Charities Toward Aid," *New York Times*, July 21, 2001, p. A10.

main function has been to act as a "civic switchboard," facilitating communication among different service providers and providing referrals on service providers to citizens. The Front Porch Alliance also acts as a liaison between the city government and the faith community. It has claimed several successful instances in which it facilitated the removal of administrative hurdles for FBO-delivered projects. In addition to its role as a community facilitator, the alliance issues grants of up to $5,000 to FBOs and other community-based organizations that provide crime prevention programs and other community services.[23]

Another example of a FBO cited as effectively serving a community is the Metropolitan Housing and Community Development Corporation (MHCDC) in Washington, North Carolina. Public officials and observers of FBOs have credited MHCDC with developing programs to address Washington's most pertinent problems, including economic depression and a high rate of HIV/AIDS patients.[24] Reverend David Moore founded the FBO, which provides a range of services to needy citizens, including a soup kitchen and shelter, classes for prospective entrepreneurs interested in starting their own businesses, and subsidized housing for elderly persons. The MHCDC also offers counseling and case management services to individuals with HIV/AIDS and their families.[25]

Many state and local officials see FBOs as particularly effective in serving rural areas. Some supporters claim they can be crucial for providing services in rural areas where they believe FBOs can supplement the financially limited resources of local government. North Carolina is one state working with FBOs to address the needs of citizens living in rural areas. The state has partnered with a nonprofit, the North Carolina Rural Economic Development Center (REDC), to improve the effectiveness of FBOs serving rural areas. The REDC focuses its outreach efforts on improving FBO financial and administrative capacity, including performance measurement capabilities. The organization is also offering demonstration grants for child care services and programs that assist welfare-to-work participants. To promote effectiveness, and to encourage further collaboration among different FBOs, the REDC awards grants only to coalitions of FBOs

---

[23] David Holmstrom, "Front Porch Alliance Fosters Church-City Cooperation in Indianapolis, City Government Connects with Religious and Community Groups," *Christian Science Monitor*, May 13, 1998, p. 12.

[24] John Manuel, "Building with Vision," *Duke Magazine*, Vol. 88, July-August 2002. Available at: [http://www.dukemagazine.duke.edu/dukemag/issues/070802/building3.html], visited Dec. 13, 2002.

[25] Dave Peterson, "Community Leadership: How One Person Can Make a Difference," June 2001, unpublished article: Raleigh, NC.

involving different religious denominations. Further, the coalitions must serve more than one county.[26]

Despite these reports, other policy makers and observers have a number of concerns about the effectiveness of FBOs, including the following:

- range of services FBOs can provide;
- lack of evaluative data on FBOs;
- qualifications of FBO personnel;
- inclusion of religious content in federally funded programs; and,
- availability of secular alternatives.

Range of Services

The Administration and other supporters have cited FBO potential to effectively deliver services in a broad range of service areas.[27] One study of FBO activities, however, found that they predominantly deliver services that address immediate, short-term needs of beneficiaries. Such services include the provision of food, housing, and clothing. The study also found that few FBOs deliver services requiring long-term face-to-face contact with beneficiaries. These more labor-intensive services include programs for health care, education (excluding religious education), substance abuse, and workforce development. Further, among the limited number of FBOs delivering long-term services, only a small fraction devote a significant amount of money and manpower to those services. The study found that FBOs delivering long-term services do not involve all their members, but rather, have a small group of volunteers that provide the service on a regular basis.[28]

Legislative Analysis and Policy Options

Currently, charitable choice provisions apply to programs in the areas of Temporary Assistance for Needy Families (TANF), substance abuse services, the Community Services Block Grant, and (to the extent they use

---

[26] Diana Jones Wilson, Director of Workforce Development, N.C. Rural Economic Development Center, telephone conversation, July 2, 2001. Also see N.C. REDC web site: [http://www.ncruralcenter.org/research/faith.htm], visited Dec. 18, 2002.

[27] White House Office of Faith-Based and Community Initiatives, *Rallying the Armies of Compassion*.

[28] Mark Chaves and William Tsitsos, *Congregations and Social Services: What They Do, How They Do It, and With Whom, Nonprofit Sector Research Fund*, The Aspen Institute, Spring 2001, pp. 12-15. Also, see generally, Avis C. Vidal, *Faith-Based Organizations in Community Development*, The Urban Institute, Prepared for the U.S. Department of Housing and Urban Development (Washington: Aug. 2001).

contracts or grants) food stamps, Medicaid, and child support enforcement. The House-passed version of H.R. 7 would have expanded charitable choice options to include nine program areas, including juvenile justice, crime prevention and victim assistance, domestic violence, GED equivalency programs,[29] after-school programs, and transit commuter programs, as well as programs funded through the Community Development Block Grant program (CDBG), Workforce Investment Act (WIA), and Older Americans Act (OAA).[30]

The CARE bill took a different approach to establishing a range of activities for FBOs. Rather than specifying federal programs, the bill sought to prevent possible discrimination against FBOs in virtually all social service programs (except education programs). The bill would have prevented federal agencies from rejecting a grant application from community-based organizations, including FBOs, because they had not previously been awarded a grant. It would also have prevented federal agencies from requiring FBOs to remove religious symbols, or alter religious provisions in charters.[31]

Given research suggesting that most FBOs deliver only short-term services, namely food, housing, and clothing, it is possible that many FBOs do not have the capacity to plan and deliver the labor-intensive, long-term services that H.R. 7 and the CARE bill proposed, and which E.O. 13279 covers. It is possible that only larger FBOs with experience administering federal grants would immediately participate in delivery of services in newly authorized program areas. Smaller FBOs with little or no experience handling federal grants might need time to gain the administrative capacity necessary to apply for and deliver federally funded services under any new program.

Both H.R. 7 and the CARE bill contained proposals for technical assistance and grants aimed at increasing the administrative capacity of FBOs. H.R. 7 would have directed the Justice Department to provide technical assistance to small nongovernmental organizations, including FBOs.[32] Similarly, the CARE bill would have authorized funds to four departments for grants and technical assistance aimed at enhancing the administrative capacity of FBOs. The CARE bill specified such activities as providing assistance with grant writing, legal assistance with incorporation

---

[29] GED programs (General Equivalency Degree) are state and local education programs offering a degree equivalent to a high school diploma.
[30] H.R. 7, Title II, sec. 1991(c)(4).
[31] S.Amdt. 4719, sec. 701.
[32] H.R. 7, Title II, sec. 1991(o).

and obtaining tax-exempt status, and information on best practices.[33] Proponents believe that technical assistance grants could enable smaller FBOs to gain the necessary capacity to deliver long-term services.

An alternative approach could be to distribute funds to state and local governments for the purpose of offering training and technical assistance to FBOs. State and local officials typically have experience administering a wide range of federal grants, which they could draw upon to train FBO personnel. In addition, if states and localities had to apply for grants, then federal assistance could potentially be directed to those jurisdictions most interested in expanding the participation of FBOs and other small nongovernmental organizations. With either approach the definition of faith-based organization could become a contentious issue.

Lack of Evaluative Data

It is sometimes said in the debate on charitable choice that there have been no rigorous, comprehensive studies on the effectiveness of services provided by FBOs, resulting in a lack of objective, quantitative evidence proving or disproving FBO effectiveness.[34] In a 1999 report on religiously affiliated nonprofits sponsored by The Aspen Institute, a nonpartisan research organization, two analysts were, "... unable to locate a single credible study assessing the relative effectiveness of religion-sponsored social services that meets the minimum requirements for evaluations." The scholars listed several potential reasons for the lack of evaluative studies, including:

- relatively little study of the nonprofit sector and its size and impact on social services;

- difficulty in evaluating performance due to the wide range of FBO-provided services and lack of service providers to compare against the FBOs;

- emergency nature of FBO-provided services, such as food and shelter programs, which may be cost-effective but are difficult to evaluate; and,

---

[33] S.Admt. 4719,, Title VIII.
[34] This observation refers to the lack of comparative evaluations and is not meant to imply that governmental agencies do not audit and evaluate FBOs and other nongovernmental providers delivering publicly funded services.

- prohibitive cost of meeting the minimum requirements for a credible program evaluation.[35]

Other scholars who specialize in the effect of religion on social problems have echoed the lack of evaluative data on FBO effectiveness. For example, Byron R. Johnson, from the Center for Research on Religion and Urban Civil Society at the University of Pennsylvania, has stated there is little reliable research proving the effectiveness of FBO-delivered programs. He further stated that there is also little evidence showing how FBO-delivered programs measure up against government-delivered programs.[36]

The Bush Administration has suggested that a lack of evaluative data should not be a reason for limiting FBO access to federal funds. In its report *Unlevel Playing Field*, it argues that there is a lack of evaluative data for all nongovernmental providers receiving federal funds, not just FBOs:

> Some critics of expended Federal collaboration with faith-based and community-based organizations complain that there is little proof that these organizations are effective or have the capacity to manage large-scale social service programs. However, as the OMB survey ironically reveals, the Federal Government routinely awards billions in taxpayer support to organizations whose own efficacy and cost-effectiveness have not been validated by careful studies. This record indicates the need for an across-the-board emphasis on demonstrating actual efficiency of the programs that government funds.[37]

Legislative Analysis and Policy Options

The first stated purpose in Title II of H.R. 7 was "to enable assistance to be provided to individuals and families in need in the most effective and efficient manner."[38] The Administration and supporters of H.R. 7 have presented a substantial amount of anecdotal information that FBOs can effectively deliver services. There have, apparently, been no comprehensive studies of FBO effectiveness or of how FBO-delivered services compare to government-delivered services. As passed by the House, Title II did not

---

[35] McCarthy and Castelli, *Religion-Sponsored Social Services*, pp. 53-54. Also see Vidal, *Faith-Based Organizations in Community Development*, pp. 3-5.

[36] Laurie Goodstein, "Church-based projects lack data on results," New York Times, April 24, 2001.

[37] White House Office of Faith-Based and Community Initiatives, *Unlevel Playing Field: Barriers to Participation by Faith-Based and Community Organizations in Federal Social Service Programs* (Washington: GPO, Aug. 2001), p. 9.

[38] H.R. 7, Title II, sec. 1991(b)(1).

require any comprehensive evaluation of the effectiveness of FBOs. This is also true of the CARE bill and E.O. 13279.

Should Congress wish to initiate an evaluation of FBOs, one possible option would be to commission a study by an independent commission or the General Accounting Office (GAO). Congress could direct that the study, to the extent possible, produce quantitative results on FBO program effectiveness, and on how FBO programs compare to government programs. Federal agencies, including those implementing the Executive Order, could be directed to report on the progress of FBO-delivered programs after a specified amount of time. An evaluation that produced objective, quantitative results might confirm or refute the anecdotal information already provided to policy makers or help to isolate and define broader problem areas.

Qualifications of FBO Personnel

Some state and local officials have expressed concern about the qualifications of FBO personnel. These officials believe that, while FBO personnel might have good intentions, they may not have the experience and skills possessed by government service providers.[39] Federal grants that provide welfare services typically include training requirements for service providers. Some public officials want to ensure that any charitable choice legislation applies the same training and skills requirements to FBOs that are applied to government agencies. The National Association of Social Workers (NASW) expressed this concern in a policy statement on the faith-based initiative: "NASW believes that all social service agencies, particularly those receiving public funding, must adhere to accreditation standards, licensing, laws, and other regulatory mechanisms that protect consumers and ensure quality service delivery."[40]

Some state and local governments actively seek to improve the qualifications of FBOs by providing training opportunities to FBOs and other community-based organizations. For example, the city of Roanoke, Virginia, coordinates a training program for organizations serving the area's homeless. The program, Homeless Educators Linking Providers and Services (HELPS), states its mission is, "To provide a forum for communication, collaboration, and coordination of services among providers for homeless and impoverished individuals and families in the Roanoke Valley." The

---

[39] Avis C. Vidal, *Faith-Based Organizations in Community Development*, pp.16-20.
[40] National Association of Social Workers, NASW Position on Faith-Based Human Services Initiatives, [http://www.socialworkers.org/advocacy/positions/faith.htm], visited Jan. 3, 2002.

program offers training opportunities to all interested service providers. Roanoke's program also focuses on raising community awareness, legislative advocacy, and improving program administration.[41]

Supporters of FBOs have suggested the use of "intermediary organizations" to assist FBO personnel in administering grant programs. These can assist FBOs with program development, grant management, financial accounting, legal services, and intergovernmental coordination. Intermediaries could also help FBOs screen and assist beneficiaries. Large nonprofit organizations most often serve as intermediaries because they typically have experience administering government funds. For-profit organizations, educational institutions, or other FBOs with grant experience may also serve as intermediaries. Some supporters of FBOs advocate using intermediaries because they can improve the capacity of smaller FBOs to deliver services.[42] With a similar goal in mind, FBOs may form coalitions to share resources and jointly provide services.[43] Virginia's faith-based liaison noted that, in its outreach programs, the state has encouraged smaller FBOs to partner with larger ones with grant experience and a greater administrative capacity.[44] Some federal agencies, including the Departments of Labor and Heath and Human Services, have made grants to intermediary groups to help FBOs improve their programs.[45]

Besides potentially improving FBOs' capacity, intermediaries can also be useful to state and local governments that wish to solicit help from the faith community, but are uncertain of how to recruit them. Some state and local governments award large grants to an intermediary, which then distributes smaller grants to FBOs to directly provide services. For example, the Department of Social Services in Los Angeles awarded a $5 million contract to Goodwill Industries, a nonprofit serving as an intermediary. Goodwill Industries then awarded grants to community-based organizations, including FBOs. One such FBO was Mobilization for the Human Family,

---

[41] Carol Wright, Human Services Coordinator, Roanoke City, VA, telephone conversation, July 2, 2001.

[42] See Oklahoma Faith-Based Liaison: [http://www.oklaosf.state.ok.us/~faithlinks/intermed.html], visited Dec. 18, 2002. Also see Kristin E. Holmes, "Faith-based Hispanic Group Has a Pioneering Role," *Philadelphia Inquirer*, Oct. 20, 2002.

[43] Paula F. Pipes and Helen Rose Ebaugh, "Faith-based Coalitions, Social Services, and Government Funding," *Sociology of Religion*, Spring 2002, pp. 49-68.

[44] Jane B. Brown, Community and Faith-Based Liaison, VA Department of Social Services, telephone conversation, July 2, 2001.

[45] Bill Broadway, "Faith-Based Groups Benefit from New Federal Grants," *Washington Post*, Aug. 3, 2002, p. B9.

which recruits, trains, and supervises volunteers who serve as mentors to recently employed TANF recipients.[46]

Legislative Analysis and Policy Options

H.R. 7 and the CARE bill did not contain provisions addressing the educational or skill level of FBO personnel that would provide services. Welfare reform legislation enacted in 1996 also contained no educational or skill requirements.[47] The only example of such a requirement in charitable choice legislation is found in the Community Renewal Tax Relief Act of 2000, which prevents states and localities from discriminating against FBOs that have received appropriate training from other FBOs.[48]

Should the 108th Congress address this issue, it might explore whether this is a problem and could clarify whether FBOs must satisfy any and all educational and skill requirements stipulated in individual grant programs. H.R. 7 and the CARE bill did not specifically instruct federal agencies, or state and local governments, to consider the qualifications of FBO personnel when evaluating FBO applications. E.O. 13279 also does not address this issue. More explicit guidance might encourage FBOs interested in applying for federal grants to improve the qualifications of their staff. On the other hand, FBOs might view such a requirement as overly stringent and might therefore be dissuaded from applying for federal funds.

Some observers were concerned that H.R. 7 provisions that exempted FBOs from Title VII of the Civil Rights Act of 1964 could affect FBOs ability to attract qualified personnel.[49] This would allow FBOs with federal funding to use religion as a factor in hiring, firing, and other personnel actions. A concern is that FBOs would place a much higher priority on religious factors than other qualifications.

Inclusion of Religious Content

One frequently debated issue in Congress's consideration of expanding FBO access to federal funds was whether or not to allow religious content in

---

[46] Amy L. Sherman, "Churches as Government Partners: Navigating 'Charitable Choice,'" *The Christian Century*, vol. 17, July 5, 2000, p. 716.

[47] P.L. 104-193, "Personal Responsibility and Work Opportunity Reconciliation Act of 1996."

[48] P.L. 106-554, sec. 584(b).

[49] H.R. 7, Title II, sec. 1991(d). For a discussion of constitutional issues and civil rights related to this exemption, see CRS Report RL31043, *Public Aid and Faith-Based Organizations (Charitable Choice): Background and Selected Legal Issues*, by David M. Ackerman.

federally funded programs.⁵⁰ Some advocates of FBOs contend that the religious component of FBO programs is the reason for their success in helping people with personal problems.⁵¹ Charitable choice provisions prohibit FBOs from requiring beneficiaries to participate in a religious program, leading some FBO supporters to fear that accepting federal funds may diminish their effectiveness. FBOs that accept federal funds and remove religious content from programs might also face challenges, possibly including diminished religious enthusiasm of FBO staff and reduction in voluntary contributions.⁵² One proponent has encouraged federally funded FBOs to offer religious activities such as Bible studies and discipleship training, but to make it clear to beneficiaries that such activities are voluntary. FBOs offering voluntary religious activities must use private funds to finance those activities. This commentator further states that beneficiaries must know they can decline to participate in religious activities without penalty.⁵³

Some interest groups representing elected and appointed public officials have established policies on faith-based initiatives that express concern over this issue. Many interest groups have suggested that charitable choice legislation should include safeguards prohibiting FBOs from including religious content in federally funded programs. The National Association of Social Workers (NASW), for example, states, "Within the faith-based initiative, safeguards must be implemented to assure that services are appropriately coordinated, provided by qualified individuals and without requirements for religious observance."⁵⁴

Legislative Analysis and Policy Options

H.R. 7 addressed the religious content issue by prohibiting FBOs from requiring beneficiaries to participate in religious activities, which some FBO

---

[50] Policy makers and observers of this issue debate the constitutionality of including religious material in federally funded programs. For a discussion of constitutional applications, please see the related CRS reports listed at the end of this report.

[51] See generally, Byron R. Johnson, "Objective Hope: Assessing the Effectiveness of Faith-Based Organizations: A Review of the Literature," Center for Research on Religion and Urban Civil Society, March 2002. Available at: [http://www.manhattan-institute.org/html/crrucs-obj_hope_press.htm], visited Dec. 18, 2002.

[52] Lewis D. Solomon and Matthew J. Vlissides, Jr., *In God We Trust? Assessing the Potential of Faith-Based Social Services*, Policy Report, Progressive Policy Institute (Washington: Feb. 2001), p. 13. See [http://www.ppionline.org/documents/FBOs_v2.pdf], visited Jan. 3, 2002.

[53] Amy L. Sherman, *The Charitable Choice Handbook for Ministry Leaders*, Center for Public Justice, 2001, p. 11.

[54] NASW, Position on Faith-Based Human Services Initiatives, 2001.

supporters believe is an essential component of their programs.[55] E.O. 13279 also includes such a requirement.[56] It is uncertain whether this requirement would encourage or discourage FBOs from applying for federal funds. On the one hand, some FBO leaders have stated that, if government funds include such provisions, they will not apply for them.[57] On the other hand, there is evidence that many FBO leaders are enthusiastic about the opportunity to apply for federal funds. Oklahoma's Office of the State Faith-Based Liaison sponsored a survey of FBOs and their willingness to collaborate with government agencies. In its survey of over 800 Oklahoma FBOs, 68% favored "receiving government funds."[58] Additionally, FBO leaders have testified before Congress that increasing FBO access to government funds will potentially improve FBO programs.[59]

There is some evidence, however, that many FBO leaders are unfamiliar with charitable choice rules. The Oklahoma survey revealed that 87% of FBO leaders considered themselves unfamiliar with charitable choice legislation and over 70% of respondents expressed concern about "possible [government] intrusion into the affairs of the congregation."[60] Another study of FBOs in Harris County, Texas, suggested that many faith-based groups are unaware of charitable choice opportunities in federal grant programs, and that many FBOs are not interested in obtaining government funds.[61]

Many supporters and opponents of the faith-based initiative have emphasized the need for FBOs to separate secular services from religious services. FBO proponent Amy Sherman, in a publication intended to explain charitable choice to ministry leaders, emphasized that, "... [F]aith-based organizations must not use government funds for purposes of 'sectarian worship, instruction, or proselytization,' and they must not require service

---

[55] H.R. 7, Title II, sec. 1991(j).
[56] E.O. 13279, sec. (2)(e).
[57] Nancy Johnson and Jessica Temple, "Faith-based Charities See Pros and Cons in Bush Proposal," *South Bend Tribune*, Feb. 4, 2001, p. 1.
[58] David P. Knudson, FaithLinks Survey, Summary of Responses, College of Continuing Education, University of Oklahoma, April 16, 2001. See the Oklahoma State Faith-Based Liaison web site: [http://www.oklaosf.state.ok.us/~faithlinks/surveyresults.pdf], visited Dec. 18, 2002.
[59] House Committee on Ways and Means, Subcommittees on Human Resources and Select Revenue Measures, *Hearing on H.R. 7, The Community Solutions Act*, hearing, 107th Congress, 1st sess., June 14, 2001. Statements of Rev. Luis Cortes, President, Nueva Esperanza Inc. and Bill Reighard, President, Food Donation Connection,(From here on referred to as Hearing).
[60] David P. Knudson, FaithLinks Survey.
[61] Pipes and Ebaugh, "Faith-based Coalitions, Social Services, and Government Funding," pp. 49-68.

recipients to participate in religious practices."⁶² A combined statement by charitable choice scholars and observers, issued by the American Jewish Committee, echoed this belief, stating, "Whenever social service programs are funded by government, or participation in such programs is mandated by government, beneficiaries have the right not to participate in religious activities."⁶³

If FBOs wish to deliver federally funded programs that satisfy constitutional requirements, it is likely that they will need to develop programs that separate federally funded services from voluntary religious activities. In this regard, a study to identify "best practices" of FBO programs might be useful. By identifying and distributing information on FBO programs that have successfully separated federally funded services from voluntary religious activities, such a study could assist other FBOs in developing programs that meet this potential requirement. Additionally, illustrating such programs might address some of the concerns of FBO leaders who are reluctant to apply for federal grants because they are uncertain how to structure their programs to comply with such a requirement.

Availability of Secular Alternatives

Another concern of some state and local policymakers is charitable choice provisions that would require governments to provide secular alternatives for services administered by FBOs, but do not provide additional federal funds for those alternative services. This requirement could potentially strain local financial resources, since governments might be placed in a position of awarding a contract to an FBO, as well as funding a secular alternative. Others have expressed concern that future reductions in federal revenues, due to tax reductions or a slowing economy, may result in less funding to social service programs, further straining the financial resources available to state and local governments to provide secular alternatives.⁶⁴ From the opposing perspective, some policy analysts and legislators believe the provision of a secular alternative to FBO-delivered services is a minimum requirement necessary to allay constitutional and

---

⁶² Amy L. Sherman, *The Charitable Choice Handbook*, p. 11.
⁶³ American Jewish Committee and Feinstein Center for American Jewish History at Temple University, *In Good Faith: A Dialogue on Government Funding of Faith-Based Social Services*, p. 8. See Pew Forum on Religion and Public Life web site: [http://www.pewforum.org/publications], visited Dec. 18, 2002.
⁶⁴ House Committee on Ways and Means, hearing, Statement of Representative Jerrold Nadler of New York.

political concerns.[65] One Member of Congress testified that, if legislation requires state and local governments to provide secular alternatives to services, but does not provide new funds, this could constitute an unfunded mandate.[66] Few state and local officials, however, have voiced strong concern about federal faith-based legislation resulting in unfunded mandates.

Legislative Analysis and Policy Options

Title II of H.R. 7, as introduced, would have required governments to provide a secular alternative for services. In the House-passed version, beneficiaries who object to the religious character of an FBO must have access to an alternate provider which is not objectionable on religious grounds.[67] By making this change, Title II arguably gave state and local governments more flexibility in providing alternative services to beneficiaries who object to the religious character of certain FBOs. If a beneficiary objects to the religious character of a FBO, the government would not necessarily have to finance an alternative service, so long as there was another service provider in the community willing and able to serve the beneficiary and whom the beneficiary did not find religiously objectionable. If a community had only religious service providers, however, and a beneficiary requested a secular one, then the government would be responsible for meeting this requirement. The CARE bill and E.O. 13279 did not address secular alternatives.

Large communities with a number of community-based organizations providing services might not have difficulty meeting such a requirement. They may be able to satisfy all beneficiaries by dividing a contract for a specific service among several service providers. Larger communities may also be able to subsidize the transport of beneficiaries to adjacent communities with acceptable providers.[68]

Although this provision may have given states and localities a degree of flexibility in providing alternative services, smaller localities with limited government resources and few community-based organizations might still have difficulty meeting such a requirement. For example, a rural locality

---

[65] OMB Watch, "Analysis of Bush Administration's Charitable Choice Initiatives," April 23, 2001, p. 7.
[66] House Committee on Ways and Means, hearing, Statement of Representative Jerrold Nadler of New York, hearing, June 14, 2001. See also U.S. Congress, House Committee on the Judiciary, *Community Solutions Act of 2001, Report to Accompany H.R. 7*, 107th Cong., 1st sess., H.Rept. 107-138, Part I (Washington: GPO, 2001), p. 300.
[67] H.R. 7, Title II, sec. 1991(g)(1) and (3).
[68] Stanley Carlson-Thies, *Charitable Choice for Welfare and Community Services: An Implementation Guide for State, Local, and Federal Officials*, Center for Public Justice, Dec., 2000, p. 21.

might award federal funds to a FBO to provide a specific service. If beneficiaries had an objection and requested an alternative provider, the local government might have difficulty financing or procuring that provider.

Policy options would be available to assist small localities with limited resources who may have difficulty meeting a requirement to provide alternative services. For the programs to which Title II of H.R. 7 would have applied, Congress could instruct federal agencies to reserve a portion of program funds to assist small communities in meeting this requirement. While such a measure might help small localities meet the requirement, it could result in a disproportionate amount of federal funds being directed to communities that contract with FBOs. Reserving program funds for this specific purpose could subtract from the overall funds used in formula allocation programs. It could also affect the cost and efficiency of service delivery.

Another option would be to leave responsibility for providing alternative services to state and local governments. Some policy-makers have expressed concern that this might be considered an unfunded mandate. The House Ways and Means Committee states in its accompanying report, however, that H.R. 7 does not impose an unfunded mandate on state and local governments.[69] Although state and local governments have not expressed concern about this issue, should legislation similar to H.R. 7 become law, state and local governments might call on Congress for assistance in satisfying the alternative services requirement.

Regarding the notification of beneficiaries of their right to alternative providers, Title II would have placed the responsibility with the appropriate federal, state, or local government.[70] If there were concern with ensuring this right, a provision could be included in statutes, regulations, or grant-making provisions requiring FBOs to notify beneficiaries. This might improve beneficiaries' awareness of the right to an alternative provider, since FBO personnel would have direct contact with the beneficiary, while government officials may not have direct contact, depending on program structure. On the other hand, monitoring such a requirement would be difficult and could lead to what some consider undue intrusion into FBO activities.

---

[69] U.S. Congress, House Committee on Ways and Means, *Community Solutions Act of 2001, Report to Accompany H.R. 7*, 107th Cong., 1st sess., H.Rept. 107-138, Part II (Washington: GPO, 2001), p. 38.
[70] H.R. 7, Title II, sec. 1991(g)(2).

Accountability for Results

In addition to providing services in an effective manner, service providers using public funds must be able to account for their results. Some public officials and observers of FBOs have concerns about the ability of FBOs to report financial and programmatic results. Some observers have suggested that a voucher system could lead to better accountability. Other observers have suggested that if FBOs separate government funds from other revenues, they would not only improve accountability, but could also better assure a separation between secular and religious activities.

FBO Ability to Report Results

Some public officials and observers of FBOs have concerns about FBOs' ability to report financial and programmatic results. One analyst stated generally of nonprofit organizations that they, "typically lack meaningful bases for demonstrating the value of what they do."[71] The National Association of Counties (NACO) addressed this concern in its resolution on the President's faith-based initiative: "There must be sufficient accountability for the use of funding, and any such programs must be coordinated within counties to maintain efficient delivery of services to the client population."[72] Historically, nonprofit organizations have sometimes resisted government efforts to modify their operations, arguing that such efforts might decrease their autonomy and ability to deliver services.[73]

Some observers of nonprofit organizations suggest that government could build public trust in nonprofit-delivered services if they are held accountable for programmatic and financial results.[74] Some state and local governments are attempting to improve the accountability of government funded FBOs in their jurisdiction. For example, North Carolina's Rural Economic Development Center, which acts as an intermediary between the state and rural FBOs, has made accountability a major criterion in its grant-making decisions. A discussion among REDC's staff and participants resulted in the following observation:

---

[71] Lester M. Salamon, *America's Nonprofit Sector* (Washington: The Foundation Center, 1999), pp. 173-175.

[72] National Association of Counties, General Resolution on the President's Initiative on Faith and Community-Based Organizations, NACO web site: [http://www.naco.org/leg/platform/resfaith01.cfm], visited Dec. 18, 2002.

[73] Salamon, *America's Nonprofit Sector*, pp. 173-175.

[74] Charles L. Glenn, *The Ambiguous Embrace: Government and Faith-Based Schools and Social Agencies* (Princeton, NJ: Princeton U. Press, 2000), p. 285.

It is essential for faith-based organizations to have the capacity to take on countywide human services, the competency to handle eligibility and case management functions, plus track their outcomes through an established monthly/annual reporting system. This means that faith-based organizations should apply for funds only if they have existing services or have spent an adequate amount of time in capacity/competency/collaborative building before launching into new territory.[75]

Other state and local governments, however, do not highly emphasize accountability. Many governments impose only minimal requirements, such as an annual report from grant recipients.[76]

Almost all federal grants have reporting requirements that include programmatic and financial results. Most long-term grants require monthly reports, while short-term project grants may only require a report upon the project's completion. All grant recipients who expend $300,000 or more in federal funds in a year undergo an audit and must satisfy the accountability standards established by OMB Circular A-133. These general reporting requirements apply to all grant recipients, whether state, local, or nonprofit agencies.[77]

Legislative Analysis and Policy Options

Title II of H.R. 7 addressed the issue of accountability by stating that FBOs receiving federal funds would be held to the same standards of accountability as secular nonprofits. The bill specifically stated "... a religious organization providing assistance under any program ... shall be subject to the same regulations as other nongovernmental organizations to account in accord with generally accepted accounting principles ...."[78] Title II further required FBOs to conduct annual self-audits and report findings to the appropriate federal, state, or local official.[79] Members of Congress who supported H.R. 7, including Representative Watts, one of the bill's sponsors, emphasized that charitable choice legislation must focus on results and insist on accountability. Some of the bill's supporters also stated that, if the federal government gives FBOs equal opportunity to compete for grants, then it must hold them equally accountable for results.[80]

---

[75] N.C. Rural Economic Development Center, Discussion Summary, Faith-Based Initiatives Conference Call, Feb. 2, 2001.
[76] Telephone conversations with selected state and local officials, June-July 2001.
[77] U.S. General Services Administration, *Catalog of Federal Domestic Assistance* (Washington: GPO, 2001), p. xviii.
[78] H.R. 7, Title II, sec. 1991(i)(1).
[79] H.R. 7, Title II, sec. 1991(i)(3).
[80] Office of Rep. Watts, Jr., H.R. 7 Community Solutions Act, Information Packet, June 2001.

H.R. 7 would have instructed the Attorney General to allocate funds for technical assistance grants to "small non-governmental organizations," including FBOs. Among the list of eligible activities for these grants, the House included information and referrals to nongovernmental organizations to provide training in accounting and program development.[81] Similarly, the CARE bill would have authorized a total of $150 million, divided among four federal departments, for grants and technical assistance to FBOs to enhance their administrative capacity. The Senate bill specified such activities as grant management training and information on best practices.[82] One option would be to add specific activities to such legislation to clarify that programmatic and financial accountability would be eligible activities under technical assistance grants. E.O. 13279 does not address reporting requirements or accountability.

Vouchers and Accountability

Some advocates of FBOs suggest using a voucher system of payment, maintaining that vouchers would allow beneficiaries to choose an organization that best suits their preferences, whether a public agency, FBO, or private agency.[83] A voucher system could also potentially improve accountability, since the organization that provides services to the most beneficiaries would receive the most federal assistance. Besides providing a surrogate performance measure, proponents believe that vouchers could offer other potential benefits, such as giving recipients greater choice in service providers and preserving the independence of FBOs. One analyst stated:

> Voucher arrangements are better than contracting for preserving the independence of faith-based organizations and giving recipients choice. Where possible, [public officials should] redesign services and procurement policies so that a range of organizations can provide services and each recipient has the chance to select the most effective and compatible provider.[84]

Opponents of the voucher approach counter that vouchers still raise concerns under the establishment clause of the Constitution, notwithstanding

---

[81] H.R. 7, Title II, sec. 1991(o)(1) and (o)(2).
[82] S. 1924, Title V.
[83] Charles L. Glenn, *The Ambiguous Embrace*, p. 285.
[84] Stanley Carlson-Thies, "Charitable Choice: Top 10 Tips for Public Officials," Center for Public Justice, 1999. See web site at: [http://downloads.weblogger.com/gems/cpj/138.pdf], visited Dec. 18, 2002.

that government assistance is not provided directly to the FBO.[85] They also argue that a voucher assumes there is a competitive marketplace for social services, when in most localities there are few, and sometimes no, providers of services. Opponents also believe vouchers hinder an organization's ability to budget effectively and plan for services.[86]

Legislative Analysis and Policy Options

The Senate's CARE bill and E.O. 13279 did not address vouchers. Title II in H.R. 7, however, would have given discretion to cabinet secretaries to determine when vouchers are a suitable payment method in particular programs.[87] Voucher payment systems, when authorized by the department secretary, might have more potential to improve accountability in more populous communities where there is a large number of service providers. In such areas, beneficiaries would have a choice of provider, which theoretically would direct the most federal funds to the most popular provider. This assumes that beneficiaries would have adequate information to make such choices, which may or may not be the case. A voucher system would have less potential to improve accountability in small communities where there may be only one service provider.

One option to address concerns would be to provide department secretaries with specific criteria for deciding when to use voucher systems. For example, Congress could craft language instructing secretaries to consider the number of service providers (both secular and religiously-affiliated) in the service area.

Separation of Government Funds

Both supporters and opponents of using FBOs have suggested that FBOs can satisfy accountability requirements and better preserve their independence and religious identity by keeping all government funds in a separate account. Religious organizations have historically been exempt from many IRS reporting requirements, unlike secular nonprofits, which are not exempt. Some observers contend that FBOs that did not separate grant funds would open themselves to public scrutiny of their religious activities, and not just their social service activities. Separated grant accounts offer a potential means of enhancing accountability while preserving the

---

[85] For more information, see CRS Report RL31043, *Public Aid and Faith-Based Organizations (Charitable Choice): Background and Selected Issues*, by David M. Ackerman.
[86] OMB Watch, "Analysis of Bush Administration's Charitable Choice Initiatives," p. 9.
[87] H.R. 7, Title II, sec. 1991(l).

independence of FBOs.[88] The Commonwealth of Virginia points out this option to FBOs, stating:

> Religious organizations contracting to provide assistance are subject to the same regulations as other service providers and will be subject to audits. If these organizations segregate Federal funds into separate accounts, only those funds will be audited. Finally, programs must be operated in compliance with federal and state laws, and funds may not be used for worship, religious instruction, or proselytizing.[89]

Legislative Analysis and Policy Options

The CARE bill did not, and E.O. 13279 does not, address separation of funds. H.R. 7, however, would have required FBOs to separate government funds they receive through grants and contracts. Only the separated government funds would be subject to audit. Further, if an FBO received government funds through vouchers it *could* separate the funds, and only separated government funds would be subject to audit.[90] These provisions would likely have enhanced the ability of federal officials to audit FBO programs. Additionally, these provisions could help allay the concerns of those officials and citizens who believe FBOs might use government funds for religious activities.

Some concerned observers stated that Congress should further improve accountability in voucher systems by requiring FBOs to separate funds received through vouchers, rather than giving them the option to separate them, as provided in H.R. 7. The point was that if the funds are not separated, then they are not subject to government audit. Requiring these funds to be separated and subject to audit would improve the ability of federal officials to audit the program. Such a requirement could result in quantitative evidence (financial records) showing that FBOs do separate federally funded services from religious activities.

The House included a provision in H.R. 7 giving states and localities discretion in co-mingling their funds with federal funds when the state or locality is contributing to a program. When states and localities co-mingle funds, all the government funds are subject to federal audit.[91] Another approach would have been to encourage those state and local governments

---

[88] OMB Watch, "Analysis of Bush Administration's Charitable Choice Initiatives,"p. 7.
[89] Virginia Community and Faith-Based Initiatives web site: [http://www.dss.state.va.us/community/291.html], visited Dec. 18, 2002.
[90] H.R. 7, Title II, sec. 1991(i)(2).
[91] H.R. 7, Title II, sec. 1991(j).

that keep their funds separated, to undertake their own audits of state and local funds.

Working Relationship Between FBOs and State and Local Governments

There is a long history of FBOs receiving funds from all levels of government to provide services. For example, in the 19th century, the federal government worked through FBOs to assist Native Americans and refugees. The "Great Society" programs of the 1960s expanded the variety of programs administered by FBOs to such areas as welfare services and community development. During the early 1980s, grants-in-aid funding was substantially reduced, but President Ronald Reagan's "New Federalism" initiative still emphasized the use of FBOs and other nonprofit organizations. One observer of FBOs and nonprofits wrote: "[They] retain a significant foothold in virtually every sphere of human service, and in many cases have been able to expand their activities as a direct by-product of government involvement."[92]

New federal legislation or initiatives to expand FBO access to federal funds could potentially disrupt good working relationships between FBOs and state and local governments. Past efforts to use community-based organizations in federal programs, whether religious or not, have sometimes produced competitive relationships between state and local governments and those community-based organizations.

This occurred, for example, in the 1960s when Congress authorized private, nonprofit agencies called Community Action Agencies (CAAs) to receive and administer federal anti-poverty funds.[93] CAAs were charged with achieving "maximum feasible participation" of community residents in the use of federal funds. During those years, some CAA officials said that their role as advocates for the poor led to adversarial relationships with local governments. Some local elected officials argued that it was inappropriate to channel federal funds away from elected governments to community organizations that were not politically accountable to the entire local electorate. As a result, CAAs and local governments sometimes competed for authority over the distribution of funds and benefits in federal

---

[92] Stephen V. Monsma, *When Sacred and Secular Mix* (Lanham, MD: Rowman & Littlefield Publishers, Inc., 1996), pp. 6-7.
[93] Economic Opportunity Act of 1964, P.L. 88-452; 78 Stat. 516.

programs.[94] In some cities, there were reports of mistrust between citizens and local officials, which led to arguably ineffective implementation of programs. For example, a CAA in Philadelphia reported:

> We only succeeded when we insisted that the politicians live up to their promises, and when we demonstrated that we had some power .... If you allow yourself to be kept busy reacting to the government's ... mountain of bureaucratic requirements, you get diverted from the really important task of initiating, refining, and acting on your community's agenda.[95]

Congress considered the views of local government officials when it created the Model Cities program in 1966, which gave local elected officials increased responsibility for certain federally funded programs.[96] Local officials, however, were required to provide "citizen participation structures [with] '... clear and direct access to the decision-making process ....'" Legislation further required local officials to provide technical assistance to community organizations administering community services.[97]

Although funding the activities of FBOs is not a new proposal, some state and local officials are concerned that increasing FBO access to federal funds could result in a similar environment of competition between FBOs and state and local governments. One community services official in Michigan also questioned whether using more FBOs could disrupt existing productive relationships between FBOs and state and local governments, as well as relationships among FBOs.[98] A representative of the American Federation of State, County and Municipal Employees (AFSCME), a public employees' union, expressed concern that the faith-based initiative, when combined with the federal tax cuts, "... will pit religious, secular nonprofit, and public agencies against each other for a declining share of federal funds ...."[99]

On the other hand, one analyst asserted that, "[c]ompetition for funds may happen, but I don't necessarily see that as a bad thing. We want the

---

[94] John H. Strange, "Citizen Participation in Community Action and Model Cities Programs," *Public Administration Review*, vol. 32, Oct. 1972., p. 660.
[95] As told to Sherry R. Arnstein, "Maximum Feasible Manipulation," *Public Administration Review*, vol. 32, Sept., 1972, p. 388.
[96] Demonstration Cities and Metropolitan Development Act of 1966, P.L. 89-754; 80 Stat. 1255.
[97] John H. Strange, "Citizen Participation," pp. 655-657.
[98] Steve Walker, Executive Director, Genesee County Community Action, quoted in Gary Heinlein, "GOP Wants Religious Groups to Take Over Welfare Tasks," *Detroit News*, Feb. 26, 2001.
[99] House Committee on Ways and Means, hearing, Statement of Nanine Meiklejohn, AFSCME.

money to go to the most efficient [organizations]."[100] Several officials from the federal, state, and local levels of government have stated that while harmful competition is possible, they are unaware of any instances in which FBOs and state and local governments have had conflicts over competition for funds or program authority.[101]

Some public officials are reporting that state-level faith-based initiatives are enhancing the relationship between FBOs and government. One Indiana state official testified to Congress that her state's FaithWorks program, "... has not created any new burden on the system or the state—rather it has helped create broadened partnerships in providing services that bring new perspectives and approaches to supporting individuals in need."[102] Other states, like Virginia, have launched awareness campaigns to communicate to FBOs the state's willingness to coordinate programs with them.

Legislative Analysis

Neither H.R. 7, the CARE bill, nor the more recent E.O. 13279, contained provisions addressing competition between FBOs and state and local governments. Charitable choice provisions like those in H.R. 7, if enacted, would likely affect the working relationship through its effectiveness and accountability provisions.

Friction between the institutions could develop if FBOs that accept government funds feel government regulations have a secularizing effect on their organization. Some FBO leaders have expressed concern over secularization, because of requirements that religious content be separated from programs receiving direct federal funding. Conversely, FBO proponent Amy L. Sherman testified before Congress that, in her interviews with FBO leaders and public officials, she found no evidence that FBOs "... felt their religious expression had been 'squelched' in their collaborative relationship with government."[103]

It is also possible that expanding charitable choice could lead to competition among FBOs. Rev. J. Brent Walker, a scholar and executive director of the Baptist Joint Committee on Public Affairs, testified before

---

[100] Steven Lazarus, Senior Policy Associate, Center for Public Justice, quoted in Gary Heinlein, "GOP Wants Religious Groups to Take Over Welfare Tasks" *Detroit News*, Feb. 26, 2001.
[101] Telephone conversations with selected federal, state, and local officials, June 2001.
[102] House Committee on Ways and Means, hearing, Statement of Katherine Humphreys, Secretary, Indiana Family and Social Services Administration.
[103] U.S. Congress, House Committee on the Judiciary, Subcommittee on the Constitution, Oversight Hearing on State and Local Implementation of Existing Charitable Choice Programs, hearing, 107th Cong., 1st sess., April 24, 1976. See House Judiciary Committee web site: [http://www.house.gov/judiciary/sherman_042401.htm], visited Jan. 3, 2001.

Congress that charitable choice "encourages unhealthful rivalry and competition among religious groups." He further expressed concern that by expanding FBO access to federal funds, the federal government could potentially be forced to choose one religious denomination over others, or at least give the impression of doing so.[104] Such a scenario is possible because U.S. citizens hold a wide range of religious beliefs. If the number of FBOs applying for federal funds increased, then federal, state, and local governments may give the perception of awarding grants to one particular denomination or FBO. Those FBOs who are not awarded funds may believe they were discriminated against on a religious basis.

CONCLUSION

In announcing his faith-based initiative, President Bush declared that "Government cannot be replaced by such organizations, but it can and should welcome them as partners."[105] A significant number of state and local government officials agree with the President that FBOs can be effective partners. On the other hand, others argue there are a number of complex institutional issues Congress should consider and resolve legislatively or through oversight of an expanded role for FBOs in the delivery of federally assisted services.

RESOURCES ON CHARITABLE CHOICE ISSUES

White House Office of Faith-Based and Community Initiatives
    [http://www.whitehouse.gov/government/fbci/]
American Civil Liberties Union
    [http://www.aclu.org/ReligiousLiberty/ReligiousLibertyMain.cfm]
Aspen Institute—Nonprofit Sector Research Fund
    [http://www.nonprofitresearch.org/index.htm]
Hudson Institute
    [http:/www.hudsonfaithincommunities.org/]
Pew Forum on Religion and Public Life
    [http://pewforum.org/]

---

[104] House Committee on Ways and Means, hearing, Statement of J. Brent Walker, Executive Director, Baptist Joint Committee on Public Affairs.
[105] U.S. President (George W. Bush), "Establishment of White House Office of Faith-Based and Community Initiatives," E.O. 13199, *Federal Register*, vol. 66, p. 8499, Jan. 31, 2001.

The Roundtable on Religion and Social Welfare Policy
[http://www.religionandsocialpolicy.org/]

Chapter 2

PUBLIC AID TO FAITH-BASED ORGANIZATIONS IN THE 107TH CONGRESS (CHARITABLE CHOICE): BACKGROUND AND SELECTED LEGAL ISSUES

David M. Ackerman

SUMMARY

Frustrated by the failure of its charitable choice proposal in the 107th Congress, the Bush Administration on December 12, 2002, announced a number of administrative initiatives to promote the involvement of religious entities in federally funded social services programs. The initiatives included an executive order extending a number of the most salient principles of charitable choice to most federally funded social services programs, a significant proposed revision in the rules governing the participation of religious organizations in the federal government's housing and community development programs, and the issuance for the first time of proposed regulations to implement existing charitable choice statutes.

The President's initiative "to rally America's armies of compassion" has been a centerpiece of his domestic program, and the Administration in the

107th Congress sought legislation providing additional tax incentives for charitable giving and extending charitable choice to most social services programs. On July 19, 2001, the House adopted a bill (H.R. 7) that, *inter alia*, would have accomplished these goals (albeit in modified form). But H.R. 7 bogged down in the Senate due to concerns about government funding of entities that employ religious faith in carrying out their programs and that discriminate on religious grounds in their employment practices. Ultimately, the Senate did not act on either H.R. 7 or on a compromise measure – the CARE Act (S. 1924) – which expanded the tax incentives of H.R. 7 but excluded most of its charitable choice provisions.

Although enacted into law in four previous statutes, charitable choice has been the subject of persistent controversy; and President Bush's initiative in the 107th Congress led the controversy to become highly visible. This report provides background and analysis on a number of the salient factual and legal issues about charitable choice in a question-and-answer format as well as an Appendix comparing the four charitable choice statutes with the House-passed version of H.R. 7 and Executive Order 13279:

(1) What is charitable choice?

(2) Aren't religious organizations already eligible to receive public funds?

(3) What charitable choice proposals have been enacted into law?

(4) What is President Bush's faith-based initiative and what steps has the Administration taken to implement it?

(5) Have any hearings been held on charitable choice?

(6) What action took place on H.R. 7 and related measures in the 107th Congress?

(7) What did the charitable choice title of H.R. 7 provide and how did it differ from previous charitable choice statutes?

(8) What legal framework governs the civil rights concerns about charitable choice?

(9) Does charitable choice violate the establishment of religion clause?

(10) What court suits involving charitable choice or similar programs have been filed or decided so far?

INTRODUCTION

In apparent response to the failure of its charitable choice legislation to pass the 107th Congress, the Bush Administration on December 12, 2002, announced a number of measures to broaden the President's faith-based initiative and to implement significant parts of the failed legislation administratively.[1] The White House

- issued an executive order (E.O. 13279) directing seven federal departments and agencies that provide financial assistance pursuant to a wide variety of social services programs to ensure that their programs conform with a number of the most salient principles of charitable choice[2];

- issued an executive order (E.O. 13280) establishing Centers for Faith-Based and Community Initiatives in the Department of Agriculture and the Agency for International Development with missions comparable to the centers previously established in five other departments[3];

- announced that the Department of Health and Human Services is, for the first time, issuing proposed regulations to implement the charitable choice provisions that have previously been enacted as part of specific grant programs;

- announced that the Department of Housing and Urban Development is issuing proposed regulations that would significantly alter its rules governing the participation of religious organizations in its housing and community development programs;

- stated that the Federal Emergency Management Agency is revising its policies to ensure that the facilities of faith-based organizations which are used for social services are eligible to receive disaster relief aid on the same basis as those of other social service organizations damaged by natural disasters;

---

[1] The announcement and the pertinent documents are available on the web site of the White House Office of Faith-Based and Community Initiatives at [[http://www.whitehouse.gov/government/fbci/]
[2] E.O. 13279, published at 67 *Fed. Reg.* 77139-44 (Dec. 16, 2002).
[3] E.O. 13280, published at 67 *Fed. Reg.* 77145-46 (Dec. 16, 2002).

- announced that the Department of Education is issuing guidelines with respect to the participation of religious organizations in providing supplemental educational services under the "No Child Left Behind Act"; and

- released a document prepared by the White House Office for Faith-Based and Community Initiatives entitled *Guidance to Faith-Based and Community Organizations on Partnering with the Federal Government* that is intended to answer some of the concerns such groups have about receiving public monies and working with the government.

These initiatives came in the aftermath of the refusal of the 107th Congress to enact any major charitable choice legislation. Soon after taking office, President Bush put forward an agenda "to enlist, equip, enable, empower, and expand the heroic works of faith-based and community groups across American."[4] That agenda included a substantial expansion of tax incentives for charitable giving and an extension of charitable choice to most of the federal government's social services programs. The House on July 19, 2001, by a vote of 233-198 adopted a modified version of that proposal (H.R. 7, the "Community Solutions Act of 2001"). But that measure bogged down in the Senate due to continuing concerns about the constitutionality and desirability of the government funding entities that employ religious faith in carrying out their programs and that discriminate on religious grounds in their employment practices. Senators Santorum (R.-Pa.) and Lieberman (D.-Conn.) developed a compromise measure early in the second session of the 107th Congress – S. 1924, the "CARE Act of 2002" – that included tax incentives for charitable giving and certain other provisions paralleling those in H.R. 7 but that excluded most of H.R. 7's charitable choice provisions. In addition, the Senate Finance Committee on July 16, 2002, reported a modified version of H.R. 7 which included tax incentives for charitable giving and other provisions paralleling those of the House-passed version and/or of S. 1924 but which excluded **all** of the charitable choice provisions of both bills. Extensive efforts were made to find an opportunity for these measures to be considered on the Senate floor along with a number of amendments by Senators critical of charitable choice. But these efforts ultimately came to naught, and the 107th Congress

---

[4] President Bush, *Rallying the Armies of Compassion* (January, 2001), available on the White House web site at www.whitehouse.gov/news/reports/faithbased.html.

adjourned on November 22, 2002, without enacting any major charitable choice legislation.

Although H.R. 7 was the major focus for debate on charitable choice in the 107th Congress, the welfare reform measure enacted in 1996 was also up for re-authorization in 2002. Charitable choice was first enacted as part of welfare reform[5]; and as a consequence, the possibility existed that the 107th Congress might revisit the issue as it revised the welfare reform program. But neither the bill adopted by the House nor the measure reported in the Senate showed any inclination to do so.[6] Ultimately, Congress postponed making any substantive revisions until early next year and simply extended the existing statute to January 11, 2003.[7]

Although enacted into law in four prior statutes,[8] charitable choice has been persistently controversial; and President Bush's initiative caused that controversy to become highly visible. Numerous aspects of charitable choice have been disputed, but much of the controversy has centered on the constitutionality and desirability of the federal government directly subsidizing faith-based social service programs and on whether subsidized religious organizations ought to be able to discriminate on religious grounds in their employment practices.

Despite the ongoing controversy about charitable choice, not until the 107th Congress were there full hearings and extended debates on its constitutionality, efficacy, and public policy implications. With particular attention to the legal issues concerning charitable choice, this report provides information and analysis on a number of factual, civil rights, and constitutional questions that have been generated. The questions it addresses are as follows:

---

[5] P.L. 104-193, Title I, § 104 (Aug. 22, 1996); 110 Stat. 2161; 42 U.S.C.A. 604a.

[6] Both the House-passed bill (H.R. 4737) and the version reported by the Senate Finance Committee would have authorized a new program to promote healthy marriages which would have been subject to the existing charitable choice rules. In addition, section 112(a)(1)(B) of the House bill directed the states to include in their state plans a description of the "strategies and programs the State is undertaking" to implement the charitable choice provisions of the 1996 statute; and § 305 of the Senate bill would have established a program of "Second Chance Homes" to provide training in parenting skills for young mothers that would be covered by the existing charitable choice rules. But neither measure would have made any change in the charitable choice rules themselves.

[7] P.L. 107-294 (November 23, 2002).

[8] These four enactments are summarized in the answer to question 3 in this report. For a fuller description of the consideration of these and other charitable choice proposals in the 104th, 105th, and 106th Congresses, see CRS Report RL30388, *Charitable Choice: Constitutional Issues and Developments Through the 106th Congress*, and CRS Report RS20712, *Charitable Choice, Faith-Based Initiatives, and TANF*.

(1) What is charitable choice?
(2) Aren't religious organizations already eligible to receive public funds?
(3) What charitable choice proposals have been enacted into law?
(4) What is President Bush's faith-based initiative and what steps has the Administration taken to implement it?
(5) Have any hearings been held on charitable choice?
(6) What legislative action took place on H.R. 7, S. 1924, and other charitable choice measures in the 107th Congress?
(7) What did the charitable choice title of H.R. 7 provide and how did it differ from previous charitable choice statutes?
(8) What is the legal framework governing the civil rights concerns that have been raised about charitable choice?
(9) Does charitable choice violate the establishment of religion clause of the First Amendment?
(10) What court suits involving charitable choice or similar programs have been filed or decided so far?

The report also includes an Appendix that compares the provisions of the four charitable choice measures that have been enacted into law, Title II of H.R. 7 as adopted by the House, and E.O. 113279. This report may be updated as events warrant.

(1) WHAT IS CHARITABLE CHOICE?

Charitable choice is a set of statutory and/or regulatory provisions intended to ensure that religious organizations can apply to participate in federally funded social services programs on the same basis as other nongovernmental providers and can provide services pursuant to such programs without abandoning their religious character or infringing on the religious freedom of recipients. The underlying assumptions of charitable choice seem to be that religious organizations should be given greater access to public funding and should be allowed to employ their faiths in carrying out the publicly funded programs to a greater degree than has traditionally been the case.[9] Except for small technical assistance programs operated by the Department of Labor and the Department of Health and Human Services,

---

[9] The latter objective may raise constitutional questions about the initiative and may also be foreclosed by certain provisions in the statutes that have been enacted as well as in H.R. 7 and in E.O. 13279. *See* the discussion under questions 8 and 9.

charitable choice does not, in itself, contain new funding for faith-based organizations. Prior to President Bush's issuance of Executive Order 13279 on December 12, 2002, charitable choice rules applied only to discrete social services programs specifically designated in four statutes enacted by Congress since 1996. The four charitable choice measures that have been enacted, the House-passed version of H.R. 7, and Executive Order 13279 differ in some of their details, and sometimes significantly so (*see* questions 4, 7, and Appendix). But the major provisions of charitable choice include the following:

(a) Protecting the Religious Character of the Organization

Charitable choice bars government from discriminating against an organization that applies to provide publicly funded social services on the basis of its religious character. To protect such organizations' religious character, charitable choice further provides that:

(i) religious organizations which receive public funds remain independent of government and retain control over the definition, development, practice, and expression of their religious belief;
(ii) government may not require such organizations to change their form of internal governance or to remove religious art and other symbols as a condition of participation; and
(iii) religious organizations which receive federal funds may discriminate on religious grounds in their employment practices as allowed under Title VII of the Civil Rights Act of 1964.[10]

The charitable choice statutes provide that a religious organization's use of public funds is subject to audit. But they allow – and in several cases require – the public funds to be segregated into a separate account and limit the government audit to that account.

(b) Protecting the Religious Freedom of Recipients

Charitable choice specifies that a religious organization cannot discriminate against a beneficiary or potential beneficiary on the basis of religion or religious belief (and in some versions on the basis of a refusal to hold a religious belief and/or a refusal to actively participate in a religious

---

[10] 42 U.S.C.A. 2000e-1.

practice as well). Charitable choice also requires that an alternate and accessible provider be made available to a recipient who objects to the religious character of a given provider and that the government give all beneficiaries notice of their right to an alternate provider. Title II of H.R. 7 as passed by the House would have added to these provisions an explicit requirement that participation by beneficiaries in any religious activity offered by a provider that receives direct governmental assistance be voluntary. But it also would have provided that this requirement of voluntariness does not apply if a religious organization receives funding indirectly, *i.e.*, in the form of vouchers; and in such programs it would have barred religious discrimination against beneficiaries only in admissions. E.O. 13279 tracks these provisions as well.

(c) Protecting the Constitutionality of the Subsidized Programs

Charitable choice bars a religious organization from using direct government aid for sectarian worship, instruction, or proselytization (unless the aid is received in the form of vouchers, in which case this restriction does not apply). Moreover, charitable choice programs are explicitly required to be implemented in a manner "consistent with" the establishment of religion clause of the First Amendment to the Constitution (and in some versions with the free exercise clause as well). Title II of H.R. 7 as passed by the House, although not the charitable choice statutes previously enacted into law, also would have required that any religious activity offered by a religious organization be separate from the program that receives direct federal assistance and that participation in any religious activity that is directly funded be voluntary for the individuals receiving services. (E.O. 13279 imposes these requirements as well.) Charitable choice also gives the government discretion with respect to whether religious programs and entities receiving federal funds have to be incorporated separately from their sponsoring religious organizations. All of these provisions, arguably, enhance the prospect that charitable choice meets constitutional requirements.

(2) AREN'T RELIGIOUS ORGANIZATIONS ALREADY ELIGIBLE TO RECEIVE PUBLIC FUNDS?

Yes. Some federal programs, such as the Child Care and Development Block Grant program,[11] explicitly specify that religious organizations are eligible to participate. More commonly, federal grant and cooperative agreement programs[12] provide that private entities or nonprofit entities are eligible to participate; and these categories include religious as well as secular organizations. Such entities as Catholic Charities USA, Lutheran Services in America, the Salvation Army, United Jewish Communities, Habitat for Humanity, and numerous other religiously affiliated or religiously sponsored organizations at the national, state, and local levels have long participated in publicly funded social services programs. These organizations are commonly incorporated separately from their sponsoring religious organizations and usually have tax-exempt status under § 501(c)(3) of the federal tax code.[13]

But interpretations and applications of the establishment of religion clause of the First Amendment as well as policy decisions by administrators have in the past generally required programs operated by religious organizations that receive direct public funding to be essentially secular in nature. Religious symbols and art have sometimes had to be removed from the premises; and religious worship, instruction, and proselytizing have been

---

[11] 42 U.S.C.A. 9858 *et seq.*
[12] "Cooperative agreement" is the legal phrase used to refer to funding agreements between the federal government and social services providers that involve substantial interaction between the government agency and the provider, while the term "grant" refers to funding agreements that do not involve substantial interaction. The term "contract" is limited to agreements for the provision of property or services to the government itself. *See* 31 U.S.C.A. 6303-6305.
[13] Section 501(c)(3) of Title 26 of the U.S. Code provides an exemption from federal income taxes to the following:

> Corporations, and any community chest, fund, or foundation, organized and operated exclusively for religious, charitable, scientific, testing for public safety, literary, or educational purposes ..., no part of the net earnings of which inures to the benefit of an private shareholder or individual, no substantial part of the activities of which is carrying on propaganda, or otherwise attempting, to influence legislation ..., and which does not participate in, or intervene in (including the publishing or distributing of statements), any political campaign on behalf of (or in opposition to) any candidate for public office.

> One of the primary benefits of tax-exempt status, and a major incentive for obtaining such status, is that donations to such organizations may be claimed as a tax deduction by the donors. *See* 26 U.S.C.A. 170.

forbidden as conditions of receiving public monies. Moreover, religious entities that have been found to be "pervasively sectarian," *i.e.*, entities in which religion is a pervasive element of all that they do, have until recently generally been deemed constitutionally ineligible to participate in most direct funding programs.

The courts have applied these constraints most strictly in the context of direct aid programs benefitting sectarian elementary and secondary schools.[14] But the same standards have been held to apply programs of direct public aid to religiously affiliated colleges and social services programs.[15] Recent decisions by the Supreme Court have loosened these constitutional constraints to a considerable degree but still require that direct public aid not be used for purposes of religious indoctrination. Charitable choice is a **legislative** and **regulatory** effort to move beyond these restrictions and to expand the involvement of religious organizations in federally-funded social services programs while allowing them at the same time to retain their religious character. (*See* question # 9 for a fuller discussion of the constitutional framework governing charitable choice.)

(3) WHAT CHARITABLE CHOICE PROPOSALS HAVE BEEN ENACTED INTO LAW?

Between 1996 and 2000 Congress enacted four charitable choice measures into law. Charitable choice was first enacted in 1996 as part of the "Temporary Assistance for Needy Families" program (TANF) and applies as well to the welfare-to-work grant program added to TANF in 1997.[16] The 105th Congress included selected charitable choice provisions in its reauthorization of the "Community Services Block Grant Program" in

---

[14] *See, e.g.,* Lemon v. Kurtzman, 403 U.S. 602 (1971) (subsidy of teachers of secular subjects in sectarian elementary and secondary schools held unconstitutional); Committee for Public Education v. Nyquist, 413 U.S. 756 (1973) (grants for maintenance and repair of sectarian school facilities and tuition subsidies for the parents of children attending private sectarian elementary and secondary schools held unconstitutional); and Wolman v. Walter, 433 U.S. 229 (1977) (public subsidy of field trip transportation for children in sectarian elementary and secondary schools held unconstitutional).

[15] *See, e.g.,* Tilton v. Richardson, 403 U.S. 672 (1971) (public subsidy of the construction of academic buildings at sectarian colleges held constitutional, subject to the restriction that the buildings be limited to secular use) and Bowen v. Kendrick, 487 U.S. 589 (1988) (provisions in Adolescent Family Life Act allowing grants to be made to religious organizations held constitutional so long as particular grants were not made to pervasively sectarian entities).

[16] P.L. 104-193, Title I, § 104 (August 22,1996); 110 Stat. 2161; 42 U.S.C.A. 604a.

1998.[17] In 2000 the 106th Congress adopted two measures adding charitable choice to the substance abuse treatment and prevention services provided under both the block grant and discretionary grant provisions of Titles V and XIX of the Public Health Services Act.[18]

The language in the 1996 welfare law has been the basic model for charitable choice. That law authorizes the states, at their option, to administer and provide TANF services or benefits through nongovernmental entities or through the provision of certificates or vouchers to TANF beneficiaries redeemable with private entities. The law said that if a state exercised this option, it had to allow religious organizations to participate on the same basis as any other private entity, subject to the requirements of charitable choice regarding the religious character of such organizations, the religious freedom of beneficiaries, and the use of funds (*see* question 1 and Appendix). Subsequent enactments and proposals have varied some of these requirements, but the basic framework of the charitable choice provisions of welfare reform has been retained.

(4) WHAT IS PRESIDENT BUSH'S FAITH-BASED INITIATIVE AND WHAT STEPS HAS THE ADMINISTRATION TAKEN TO IMPLEMENT IT?

(a) Initial Effort

The promotion of increased involvement by faith-based and community organizations in federally funded social services programs has been a centerpiece of President's Bush's domestic agenda. Soon after taking office, on January 29, 2001, President Bush issued two executive orders establishing federal offices to define and promote this initiative. Executive Order 13199 created an Office of Faith-Based and Community Initiatives in the White House to take the lead responsibility in enhancing and promoting

---

[17] P.L. 105-285, Title II, § 201 (Oct. 27, 1998); 112 Stat. 2749; 42 U.S.C.A. 9920.
[18] P.L. 106-310, Title XXXIII, § 3305 (Oct. 17, 2000); 114 Stat. 1212; 42 U.S.C.A. 300x-65 (West Supp. 2001) and P.L. 106-554, § 1 (Dec. 21, 2000); 114 Stat. 2763; 42 U.S.C.A. 290kk (West Supp. 2001). The charitable choice provisions in the latter act were part of H.R. 5662, the "Community Renewal Tax Relief Act of 2000," which was incorporated and enacted by reference in the "Consolidated Appropriations Act, 2001." *See* 114 Stat. 2763I-1, at 2763I-33.

governmental partnerships with faithbased and community organizations.[19] Executive Order 13198, in turn, established centers for faith-based and community initiatives in each of five federal agencies – the Departments of Health and Human Services, Housing and Urban Development, Labor, Justice, and Education.[20] These centers are mandated to work with the White House office in order to make their agencies "as open and supportive as possible to successful faith-based and grassroots organizations" and, more particularly, to identify and eliminate regulatory, statutory, and administrative barriers to the participation of such groups. On August 16, 2001, the White House issued the first of what it said will be annual reports summarizing the initial findings of the departmental centers – *Unlevel Playing Field: Barriers to Participation by Faith-Based and Community Organizations in Federal Social Service Programs*.[21]

These executive orders were part of a document released by President Bush on January 30, 2001, entitled *Rallying the Armies of Compassion*. The document detailed his agenda "to enlist, equip, enable, empower, and expand the heroic works of faith-based and community groups across America" and set forth the following initiatives:

- encouraging and helping states to create their own versions of the White House Office of Faith-Based and Community Initiatives;

---

[19] 66 Fed. Reg. 8499 (Jan. 31, 2001). Initially, that office was headed by Catholic scholar John J. DiIulio, Jr. But on August 17, 2001, the White House announced his resignation. On February 2, 2002, President Bush announced the selection of James Towey, an attorney with an extensive background in working with social services organizations, as the head of the office and also designated him as a Deputy Assistant to the President.

[20] *Id.* at 8497.

[21] The report summarized the initial findings of the five departmental centers as including the following:

    (i)   small faith-based and secular groups receive "very little" federal support relative to the scope of the services they provide;

    (ii)   there is a "widespread bias" against such groups reflected in "cumbersome" regulations and prohibitions on religious activities that go beyond constitutional requirements;

    (iii) regulations often impose requirements beyond what the legislation mandates;

    (iv) the existing charitable choice statutes have been "almost entirely ignored" by federal administrators;

    (v)   there is very little evaluation of the results that are achieved in federally funded social services programs; and

    (vi) the Government Performance and Results Act of 1993, which was enacted to promote performance-based management, has had "little discernible impact."

The report is available on the White House web site at [http://www.whitehouse.gov/news/releases/2001/08/unlevelfield.html]

- a commitment to fully implement the charitable choice measures that have previously been enacted into law;

- a recommendation that pilot programs incorporating charitable choice be established to help the children and families of prisoners, to improve inmate rehabilitation prior to release, to establish maternity group homes, and to provide after-school programs for low-income children; and

- an expansion of incentives for private giving to religious and charitable enterprises by such means as allowing a charitable gift tax deduction to those who do not itemize on their federal income tax returns, permitting individuals to take tax-free withdrawals from their IRAs for the purpose of making charitable contributions, limiting the liability of corporations for the donation of equipment and supplies to charitable organizations, encouraging the states to adopt a charitable gift tax credit, increasing the charitable donation deduction for corporations from 10 percent to 15 percent of taxable income, and creating a Compassion Capital Fund from both federal and private funds to provide technical assistance to small community and faith-based organizations and to provide start-up capital to such enterprises.

In the 107th Congress the Administration strongly supported H.R. 7, the "Community Solutions Act of 2001," as the primary legislative vehicle for a number of these initiatives.[22] When that bogged down in the Senate, President Bush heralded the bipartisan compromise worked out by Sen. Lieberman and Sen. Santorum (S. 1924) as "a great accomplishment" and urged its adoption, notwithstanding its deletion of most of the charitable choice provisions in the House bill.[23] The 107th Congress adjourned without either measure coming up for Senate floor action, however.

Nonetheless, pieces of the proposals listed above have been enacted as parts of other legislation. For instance, the fiscal 2002 appropriations act for the Departments of Justice, Commerce, and State[24] included a directive that $5 million be used to start five faith-based pilot programs in prisons to help

---

[22] As noted above, S. 584 was originally the Senate counterpart to H.R. 7. Like S. 1924, that measure also did not include the charitable choice title or the corporate liability reform provisions of H.R. 7. It was superseded by S. 1924 and the version of H.R. 7 reported by the Senate Finance Committee.

[23] White House Office of the Press Secretary, "Remarks by the President and Senator Lieberman in Photo Opportunity After Meeting on Armies of Compassion" (Feb. 7, 2002).

inmates prepare for release.[25] Similarly, the fiscal 2002 appropriations act for the Departments of Labor, Health and Human Services, and Education and Related Agencies provided $30 million to the Department of Health and Human Services (HHS) to establish a Compassion Capital Fund "to provide grants to charitable organizations to emulate model social service programs and to encourage research on the best practices of social service organizations."[26] HHS is using the funds to support intermediary organizations that can help faith-based and community-based organizations to compete for funding, partner with other organizations, and replicate and implement best practices in program management and service.[27] The fiscal 2003 appropriations bill as reported in the Senate (but not enacted by the 107th Congress) included $45 million for this Compassion Capital Fund,[28] while the bill as introduced in the House (H.R. 5320) would have provided $100 million. As a final example, President Bush on January 17, 2002, signed into law a new authorization of $67 million to provide mentoring services to children of prisoners.[29]

(b) The December 12, 2002, Initiative

As noted above, the 107th Congress adjourned on November 22, 2002, without enacting any major charitable choice legislation. In apparent response to that fact, and to further implement the President's faith-based initiative, the White House on December 12, 2002, announced a number of significant administrative actions, as follows:

---

[24] P.L. 107-77 (Nov. 28, 2001).
[25] The allocation was made by language in the legislative history of the statute. In H. Rept. 107-139, 107th Cong., 1st Sess. (July 13, 2001), at 35, the House Appropriations Committee stated as follows:

> In addition, the Committee supports the request to establish a multi-faith based prison pre-release pilot program. The Committee directs that a fifth pilot be added, and that it be located at the Petersburg, VA, facility.

The conference report on the legislation, in turn, stated that "[t]he conference adopts by reference House language regarding drug treatment programs and establishment of faith-based and other pilots ...." *See* H. Conf. Rept. 107-278 (Nov. 9, 2001), *reprinted at* 147 CONG. REC. H 8008 (daily ed. Nov. 9, 2001).

[26] P.L. 107-116, Title II (Jan. 10, 2002); 115 Stat. 2177, 2196.
[27] 67 Fed. Reg. 39561-39570 (June 7, 2002).
[28] S. 2766, as reported by the Senate Appropriations Committee on July 22, 2002 (S. Rept. 107-206).
[29] P.L. 107-133, Title I, Subpart B (Jan. 17, 2002); 115 Stat. 2413, 2419; 42 U.S.C.A. 629i.

(1) Executive Order 13280 – Establishment of New Centers[30]

By an earlier executive order (E.O. 13198) the President on January 31, 2001, established Offices of Faith-Based and Community Initiatives in five federal departments – Health and Human Services, Housing and Urban Development, Labor, Justice, and Education. This new executive order (E.O. 13280) establishes similar offices in the Department of Agriculture and the Agency for International Development. Like their predecessors, these new offices are charged with identifying barriers to the participation of faith-based and community organizations in their social services programs, removing such barriers, encouraging the participation of such organizations "to the greatest extent possible," developing innovative programs to increase their participation, and expanding outreach efforts to them.

(2) Executive Order 13279 – Equal Protection of the Laws for Faith-Based and Community Organization[31]

By this executive order the President is directing the heads of the aforementioned seven departments and agencies to ensure that the regulations and policies governing the administration of their social services programs conform with several of the major principles of charitable choice. The scope of the executive order is broad. It applies to social services programs administered directly by the seven departments and agencies or by state and local governments using federal financial assistance provided under their programs; and the programs covered include those "directed at reducing poverty, improving opportunities for low-income children, revitalizing low-income communities, empowering low-income families and low-income individuals to become self-sufficient, or otherwise helping people in need."[32] The executive order directs that the administration of these social services programs conform with the following principles of charitable choice:

- Faith-based and other community organizations should be able "to compete on an equal footing for Federal financial assistance" with all other eligible organizations.

---

[30] 67 Fed. Reg. 77145 (Dec. 16, 2002).
[31] 67 Fed. Reg. 77139-44 (Dec. 16, 2002).
[32] The executive order states that such programs include, but are not limited to, child care services; transportation services; job training; referral and counseling services; health support services; soup kitchens and food banks; literacy and mentoring programs; the prevention of juvenile delinquency, crime, substance abuse, and domestic violence; and housing.

- "No organizations should be discriminated against on the basis of religion or religious belief in the administration or distribution of Federal financial assistance ...."

- All organizations that receive federal financial assistance under the social services programs of these seven departments and agencies should be barred from discriminating "against current or prospective program beneficiaries on the basis of religion, a religious belief, a refusal to hold a religious belief, or a refusal to actively participate in a religious practice."

- In order to comply with the establishment and free exercise clauses of the Constitution, organizations that engage in "inherently religious activities, such as worship, religious instruction, or proselytization, must offer those services separately in time or location from any programs or services supported with direct Federal financial assistance, and participation in any such inherently religious activities must be voluntary for the beneficiaries" of programs that are directly subsidized.

- Religious organizations that participate in federally financed social service programs may not "use direct Federal financial assistance to support any inherently religious activities, such as worship, religious instruction, or proselytization."

- Faith-based organizations that apply for or participate in federally financed social service programs may "retain [their] independence and ... continue to carry out [their] mission, including the definition, development, practice, and expression of [their] religious beliefs; use their facilities to provide social services "without removing or altering religious art, icons, scriptures, or other symbols"; retain religious terms in their names; select board members on a religious basis; and include religious references in their "mission statements and other chartering or governing documents."

With the exception of an amendment to another existing order concerning federal procurement, E.O. 13279 is silent with respect to discrimination on religious grounds in the employment practices of religious organizations.[33] Executive Order 13279 gives the departments and agencies 90 days to develop implementation plans.

(3) Regulations To Implement Existing Charitable Choice Statutes

The Department of Health and Human Services (DHHS) on December 12, 2002, issued proposed rules to implement the four charitable choice statutes enacted into law between 1996 and 2000.[34] No such regulations have previously been provided. The proposed regulations would apply to the Temporary Assistance for Needy Families program (TANF) under the Personal Responsibility and Work Opportunity Reconciliation Act of 1996, the Community Services Block Grant program, the substance abuse prevention and treatment block grant and discretionary grant programs administered by the Substance Abuse and Mental Health Services Administration (SAMHSA), and the Projects for Assistance in Transition from Homelessness grant program (also administered by SAMHSA). All of the proposed regulations incorporate **all** of the principles set forth above in Executive Order 13279. All have the following additions as well:

- Although E.O. 13279 states that faith-based organizations that receive *direct* federal financial assistance cannot use the assistance for inherently religious activities, all of the proposed regulations emphasize that this restriction does *not* apply to federal financial assistance that is received *indirectly, i.e.*, funding that an organization receives "as the result of the genuine and independent private choice of a beneficiary through a voucher, certificate, coupon, or other similar mechanism." Thus, the proposed regulations explicitly affirm that organizations that receive funds indirectly can use them for inherently religious activities and need not segregate their religious activities by time or location from the subsidized activities.

- All of the proposed regulations explicitly state that receipt of funds under the applicable program by a religious organization does not

---

[33] Executive Order 13279 amends E.O. 11246 to specify that religious organizations that contract to provide goods or services directly to the federal government can discriminate on religious grounds in their employment practices. E.O. 11246 has no direct relevance to the social service programs that are otherwise the subject of E.O. 13279.

[34] *See* 67 Fed. Reg. 77349-60 (SAMHSA programs), 77361-67 (TANF program), and 77368-71 (Community Services Block Grant program) (Dec. 17, 2002). The proposed regulations are also available at the website of the DHHS Office of Faith-Based and Community Initiatives: [http://www.hhs.gov/fbci/]

affect the organization's exemption from the religious nondiscrimination in employment requirement of Title VII of the Civil Rights Act of 1964.[35] In other words, participating religious organizations can discriminate on religious grounds in their employment practices as allowed under Title VII notwithstanding their receipt of public funds. The regulations applicable to the programs administered by or through SAMHSA further state that the religious nondiscrimination in employment requirements in the Public Health Service Act[36] also do not apply if a participating religious organization can demonstrate that application of the requirement would "substantially burden" its religious exercise. The reason for that exception, the explanatory material states, is not anything in charitable choice but the Religious Freedom Restoration Act,[37] which bars the federal government from imposing any "substantial burden" on religious exercise unless necessary to accomplish a compelling public purpose.

- All of the proposed regulations state that beneficiaries who object to the religious character of a given service provider have a right to receive services from another provider to whom they have no religious objection. The regulations require that beneficiaries be given notice of their right to an alternative provider, that such alternative providers be "reasonably accessible," and that the value of the services received be no less than those that would have been received from the original provider. The regulations further make clear that the alternative provider need not be non-religious, just non-objectionable on religious grounds to the beneficiary.

(4) Revision of DHUD's Housing and Community Development Regulations

On December 12, 2002, the Department of Housing and Urban Development (DHUD) announced that it would soon publish proposed regulations that would substantially revise its rules governing the participation of religious organizations in several housing and community

---

[35] 42 U.S.C.A. 2000e-2.
[36] 42 U.S.C.A. 290cc-33(a)(2) and 300x-57(a)(2) (West Supp. 2002) of the Public Health Service Act provide that "[n]o person shall on the ground of sex ... or ... religion be excluded from participation in, be denied the benefits of, or be subjected to discrimination under, any program or activity funded in whole or in part with funds made available under section ... of this title."
[37] 42 U.S.C.A. 2000bb *et seq.*

development programs – the Community Development Block Grant (CDBG) program; HOME Investment Partnerships program; Hope for Homeownership of Single-Family Homes; Housing Opportunities for Persons with AIDS; Emergency Shelter Grant program; Shelter Plus Care; Supportive Housing; and Youthbuild.[38] Existing regulations allow religious organizations to participate but impose special restrictions on "primarily religious" entities. More particularly, existing regulations generally (1) prohibit direct assistance to primarily religious organizations for the construction, acquisition, or rehabilitation of housing or other structures; (2) require such entities, in order to obtain grants for the acquisition, construction or rehabilitation of housing or other structures, to form separate secular corporations; and (3) require that structures constructed, acquired, or rehabilitated with public funds be used for wholly secular purposes. In addition, existing regulations governing the receipt of grants by primarily religious organizations for the provision of services generally bar them from (4) discriminating on religious grounds in their employment practices and (5) exerting "religious influence" in their provision of services. The proposed regulations would eliminate all of these requirements. In other words, grants could be made directly to primarily religious organizations for all purposes; such entities would not need to set up separate secular organizations to receive grants for the construction, acquisition, or rehabilitation of housing or other structures. Moreover, structures constructed, acquired, or rehabilitated with public funds could be used not only for eligible secular activities but also for inherently religious ones; public funding in such situations would simply have to be limited to the proportion for which the structures are used for eligible activities. Finally, religious entities receiving public funds could discriminate on religious grounds in their employment practices.

The proposed regulations would also incorporate all of the charitable choice principles described above in Executive Order 13279.

(5) Practical Guidance

To facilitate the participation of faith-based and community organizations in federally funded social services programs, the White House Office of Faith-Based and Community Initiatives on December 12, 2002, issued a brochure entitled *Guidance to Faith-Based and Community*

---

[38] The existing regulations for these programs are found at 24 CFR Part 92, 570, 572, 574, 576, 582, 583, and 585, respectively.

Organizations on Partnering with the Federal Government.[39] The brochure provides general information on the federal grant process and specific information on a list of "do's and don't" for faith-based organizations. The latter section addresses such questions as whether religious organizations need to form a separate nonprofit corporation to receive public funds and whether funded entities can engage in religious activities, discriminate on religious grounds in their employment practices, or discriminate on religious grounds in providing services. The brochure is organized in a question and answer format and generally elaborates in colloquial language the charitable choice principles set forth in Executive Order 13279. But it also provides specific answers to questions that are only implicitly addressed by the executive order.

(6) Eligibility for Disaster Assistance

The White House and the Federal Emergency Management Agency (FEMA) announced on December 12, 2002, that FEMA is revising the standards governing the eligibility of certain private, nonprofit organizations for assistance to repair damage caused by natural disasters. The White House announcement stated that "[u]nder current FEMA policy religious non-profits such as schools, soup kitchens, and homeless shelters cannot receive federal disaster relief when they suffer damage" and that "[u]nder the changes announced by the President today, faith-based social service organizations will be eligible to receive aid just like other social service organizations damaged or destroyed by natural disasters, retroactive to January 2001." The FEMA announcement stated that "this new policy will recognize the eligibility of the Seattle Hebrew Academy (SHA), a religious school closed for almost two years due to damages suffered during the Nisqually, Washington earthquake on February 28, 2001."

(5) HAVE ANY HEARINGS BEEN HELD ON CHARITABLE CHOICE?

Notwithstanding the enactment of four charitable choice measures in the 104th, 105th, and 106th Congresses, no congressional committee had held a hearing on charitable choice prior to the first session of the 107th Congress. In the 107th Congress five hearings were held, as follows:

---

[39] The brochure is available on the web site of the White House OFBCI: [http://www.whitehouse.gov/government/fbci/guidance_document.pdf]

(1) Two hearings were held by the Subcommittee on the Constitution of the House Judiciary Committee, chaired by Rep. Chabot (R.-Oh). The first, on April 24, 2001, examined "State and Local Implementation of Existing Charitable Choice Programs." The second, on June 7, 2001, focused on "The Constitutional Role of Faith-Based Organizations in Competitions for Federal Social Service Funds."[40]

(2) On April 26, 2001, the Subcommittee on Criminal Justice, Drug Policy, and Human Resources of the House Committee on Government Reform, chaired by Rep. Souder (R.-Ind.) held a hearing on "The Role of Community & Faith-Based Organizations in Providing Effective Social Services."[41]

(3) On June 6, 2001, the Senate Committee on the Judiciary, chaired by Sen. Leahy (D.-Vt.), held a hearing on "Faith-Based Solutions: What Are the Legal Issues?"[42]

(4) On June 14, 2001, two subcommittees of the House Ways and Means Committee – the Subcommittee on Human Resources, chaired by Rep. Herger (R.-Ca.), and the Subcommittee on Select Revenue Measures, chaired by Rep. McCrery (R.-La.) – held a joint hearing on H.R. 7 as introduced in the House.[43]

---

[40] *State and Local Implementation of Existing Charitable Choice Programs: Hearing Before the Subcommittee on the Constitution of the House Committee on the Judiciary*, 107th Cong., 1st Sess. (April 24, 2001) (Serial 107-13) and *The Constitutional Role of Faith-Based Organizations: Hearing Before the Subcommittee on the Constitution of the House Committee on the Judiciary*, 107th Cong., 1st Sess. (June 7, 2001) (Serial 107-17).

[41] *The Role of Community and Faith-Based Organizations in Providing Effective Social Services: Hearing Before the Subcommittee on Criminal Justice, Drug Policy, and Human Resources of the House Committee on Government Reform*, 107th Cong., 1st Sess. (April 26, 2001) (Serial 107-69).

[42] *Faith-Based Solutions: What Are the Legal Issues?: Hearing Before the Senate Committee on the Judiciary*, 107th Cong., 1st Sess. (June 6, 2001) (S. Hrg. 107-375) (Serial No. J-107-24).

[43] *H.R. 7 -- The Community Solutions Act of 2001: Hearing Before the Subcommittee on Human Resources and the Subcommittee on Select Revenue Measures of the House Committee on Ways and Means*, 107th Cong., 1st Sess. (June 14, 2001) (Serial 107-34).

(6) WHAT LEGISLATIVE ACTION OCCURRED ON H.R. 7, S. 1924, AND OTHER CHARITABLE CHOICE MEASURES IN THE 107TH CONGRESS?

(a) H.R. 7, the "Community Solutions Act of 2001," and S. 1924, the "CARE Act of 2002"

As noted above, H.R. 7, the "Community Solutions Act of 2001," was the primary initiative concerning charitable choice in the 107th Congress but was not ultimately enacted. The bill was introduced with the support of the White House on March 29, 2001, by Rep. Watts (R.-Okla.), Rep. Hall (D.-Oh.), and Speaker Hastert (R.-Ill.).[44] The measure included not only an expansion of charitable choice but also tax incentives for charitable giving, limitations on corporate liability for charitable donations of equipment, and modifications of the program of individual development accounts for low-income persons. The tax incentive provisions of Title I and the individual development account provisions of Title III were referred to the Committee on Ways and Means, while the corporate liability provisions of Title I and the charitable choice provisions contained in Title II were referred to the Committee on the Judiciary. After an all-day markup session on June 28, 2001,[45] the Judiciary Committee approved, 20-5, a substitute version of the corporate liability and charitable choice sections offered by its chairman, Rep. Sensenbrenner (R.-Wis.), which had been developed in extensive discussions with the Administration. The Democratic minority proposed numerous modifications to the substitute, but most of these were rejected.[46]

---

[44] An identical bill, H.R. 1284, was introduced by the same sponsors on March 28, 2001.

[45] The transcript of the Committee's markup is reproduced in the committee's report on H.R. 7, *infra*, n. 23.

[46] *See* H. Rept. 107-138, Part I, 107th Cong., 1st Sess. (July 12, 2001). As noted, the report includes a transcript of the markup. Amendments rejected by the committee included

  (i) proposals by Rep. Scott (D.-Va.) to strike the Title VII exemption allowing religious organizations to discriminate on religious grounds in their employment practices (11-19), to exclude all ESEA programs from the purview of charitable choice (10-17), to require an alternative provider to be "at least as accessible" as the original provider (voice vote), to define a religious organization as a "pervasively sectarian" entity (voice vote), and to require funding decisions to be made on the basis of the "objective merits of the applications submitted" (7-20);
  (ii) proposals by Rep. Nadler (D.-N.Y.) to broaden the judicial relief provision by allowing suits against religious organizations as well as governmental agencies and permitting the award of damages as well as injunctive relief (voice vote); to require as a condition of eligibility that a religious organization be incorporated separately

The Ways and Means Committee, in turn, marked up the tax and individual development account provisions on July 11, 2001, and approved a version substantially reducing the amount of the tax incentives by a vote of 23-16.[47] On July 19, 2001, the House debated a substitute proposal proffered by Rep. Sensenbrenner that combined and slightly modified the foregoing measures, rejected two minority proposals, and adopted the substitute, 233-198.[48]

In the Senate H.R. 7 failed to garner widespread support and languished in the Senate Finance Committee As a consequence, Senators Santorum (R.-Pa.) and Lieberman (D.-Conn.) developed and introduced a bill (S. 1924) on February 8, 2002, that provided more generous tax incentives than H.R. 7, comparable individual development account provisions, and a restoration of the full amount of the social services block grant. But S. 1924 excluded *most* of the charitable choice provisions of H.R. 7. Subsequently, on July 16, 2002, the Senate Finance Committee reported out a version of H.R. 7 that incorporated many of the tax incentive and individual development account provisions of S. 1924 but that had *none* of the charitable choice provisions of the House-passed measure or even the more modest provisions concerning

---

from its pervasively sectarian parent or affiliate (voice vote), to bar a religious organization from engaging any beneficiary in religious activity while that person is receiving assistance (7-22), and to require that a secular alternative provider be provided to an individual who objected to the religious character of an initial provider (voice vote);

(iii) a proposal by Rep. Frank (D.-Mass.) to bar religious organizations receiving assistance indirectly from discriminating against an individual on the basis of a religious belief (7-15);

(iv) a proposal by Rep. Lofgren (D.-Cal.) to strike the liability reform section concerning corporate donations to charitable organizations (7-13); and

(v) a proposal by Rep. Jackson-Lee (D.-Tex.) to strike the section concerning the autonomy of religious organizations (7-19).

Amendments accepted by the committee included one by Rep. Scott to increase the authorization for technical assistance to $50 million and to allow such assistance to include help in creating a 501(c)(3) organization (accepted by unanimous consent) and another to add a provision to the subsection stating that funds are not to be considered aid to the religious organization saying that Title VI still applies (voice vote); a modified amendment by Rep. Watt stating that religious organizations that receive public funds, notwithstanding their partial exemption from Title VII, still must comply with its nondiscrimination provisions (accepted by unanimous consent); and an amendment by Rep. Frank stating that nothing in the section alters the duty of a religious organization to comply with Title VI, Title IX, section 504, and the Age Discrimination Act of 1975 (voice vote).

[47] *See* H. Rept. 107-138, Part II, 107th Cong., 1st Sess. (July 16, 2001). The committee reduced the cost of the tax incentives for charitable giving from the $84.4 billion originally proposed to $6.4 billion (estimated over ten years). *See* Congressional Quarterly, *Ways and Means Scales Back Bush Plan for Fostering Charitable Donations* (July 14, 2001), at 1688.

[48] 147 CONG.REC. H4222 - H4281 (daily ed. July 19, 2001).

religious organizations of S. 1924.[49] Senators Santorum and Lieberman led efforts to develop a unanimous consent agreement that would have allowed H.R. 7 and the excluded provisions of S. 1924 as well as several amendments by opponents of charitable choice to be considered on the Senate floor. But the 107th Congress came to an end without any Senate floor debate on charitable choice on either H.R. 7 or S. 1924. The following subsections give greater detail on what happened on these measures:

(i) Judiciary Committee Report

In reporting the bill on July 12, 2001, the Judiciary Committee stressed that charitable choice is "not new" and has previously been enacted four times. It stated that the bill was a response to the decline in private philanthropy caused by "higher and higher taxes" as well as to "misguided understandings of the Constitution" which prevented government from working more closely with religious organizations; that support for public funding of social services programs operated by religious organizations was strong, "particularly ... among African-Americans"; that "[e]xisting charitable choice programs have had a significant impact on social welfare delivery"; and that H.R. 7 had been modified to respond to some of the criticisms that had been made about charitable choice.

The report also gave an extended defense of the constitutionality of charitable choice and of the provision allowing religious organizations to discriminate on religious grounds in their employment practices. It emphasized that the bill ensured that aid to social services organizations would be distributed in a religiously neutral way and that it respected the "individual choices, whether religious or nonreligious, of the needy who are served by these programs." Recent decisions by the Supreme Court, it said, had abandoned the notions that public aid cannot be provided directly to pervasively sectarian organizations and that employees of such organizations "cannot be trusted to follow guidelines preventing the use of Government funds for proselytizing activities ...." The bill, it said, contained "constitutionally adequate safeguards" for monitoring how public funds are used. Moreover, with respect to the new provision in H.R. 7 authorizing social services programs to be converted to voucher programs if deemed "feasible and efficient" by the Secretary of the administering department, the report asserted that "[c]haritable choice programs administered through the use of vouchers or certificates to individuals, who may then choose to give

---

[49] *See* S. Rept. 107-211 (July 16, 2002).

them to nonreligious or religious organizations in return for services, enjoy the widest constitutional berth":

> So long as the initial beneficiaries have a choice about where to redeem the vouchers or certificates, and a range of choices are available including religious and nonreligious social service organizations, such programs do not violate the First Amendment.[50]

With respect to employment discrimination, the committee report contended that "one of the most important charitable choice principles is the guarantee of institutional autonomy that allows faith-based organizations to select staff on a religious basis .... This guaranteed ability is central to each organization's freedom to define its own mission according to the dictates of its faith." That is the reason, the report stated, that Congress wrote an exemption for religious organizations into Title VII of the Civil Rights Act of 1964; and that exemption, it asserted, "is not waived or forfeited when a religious organization receives Federal funding." "Staffing on a religious basis," it said, does not constitute "invidious discrimination; and constitutionally the exemption is a "permissible religious accommodation." Moreover, it stated, this exemption should apply "even when State or local laws provide otherwise." Both the autonomy provision and the provision stating that the charitable choice rules apply to state funds that are commingled with federal funds, the report stated, served to preempt state and local civil rights laws that would intrude on the right of religious organizations to employ persons of their own faiths. The report noted that under H.R. 7 the right is judicially enforceable.

Twelve Democrats filed "Dissenting Views" in the committee report stating that "[w]e cannot support legislation which seeks to enlarge the role of religious institutions by sanctioning government-funded discrimination and by breaking down the historic separation between church and state." Contending that the bill not only allowed religious organizations to discriminate on the basis of a prospective employee's religion but also on the basis of "a failure to adhere to religious doctrine (*e.g.*, being pregnant and unmarried, being gay or lesbian)" and that it preempted conflicting state and local nondiscrimination laws as well, the dissenters asserted that "it is unacceptable for any group or entity to discriminate with taxpayer funds." Given that the federally funded services to be provided by such organizations must be wholly secular under H.R. 7, they said, employment discrimination on the basis of religion is simply unnecessary.

---

[50] H. Rept. 107-38, Part I, *supra*, at 28.

With respect to the separation of church and state, the dissenters contended that the safeguards in the bill were inadequate. They noted that H.R. 7 provided no funds to ensure that a beneficiary's right to a secular alternative to a faith-based service – "the most critical Establishment Clause safeguard included in the legislation" – could be honored and said the requirement constituted "an unfunded and unenforceable mandate." They contended as well that the other "key religious protections in the bill" – the ban on the use of government funds for sectarian proselytization and the requirements that religious activity be separate from the funded program and that participation in such activity be voluntary -- were "largely left to self enforcement." They questioned as well whether participation in such programs by children or, perhaps, even drug addicts could ever be truly voluntary. The dissenters further argued that the nondiscrimination provisions in the bill still allowed religious organizations to discriminate not only on grounds of religion but also on the grounds of "sex, pregnancy status, marital status, or sexual orientation." Moreover, they asserted, in indirectly funded programs the ban on religious discrimination applied only to admissions and the requirements that religious activities be separate and voluntary did not apply at all. The dissenters further charged that the funding process contemplated by H.R. 7 would diminish religion's "independent voice of compassion," support only those religious groups able to muster sufficient lobbying power to obtain government grants, precipitate intense religious competition for funds, and lead to government discrimination against unpopular groups. Finally, the dissenters expressed "concern that H.R. 7 would fail to pass constitutional muster."

(ii) Rules Committee Report

On July 17, 2001, the House Rules Committee adopted a rule which provided that in lieu of the bill as reported by the two committees, a substitute amendment sponsored by Rep. Sensenbrenner which consolidated and reordered their recommendations would be deemed the pending bill upon adoption of the rule.[51] The rule also made in order a minority substitute measure that proposed to (1) delete the Title VII exemption allowing religious organizations to discriminate on grounds of religion in their employment practices, (2) add a provision making clear that state and local civil rights laws remain applicable to religious organizations receiving funds

---

[51] *See* H. Rept. 107-144, 107th Cong., 1st Sess. (July 17, 2001), accompanying H. Res. 196. The Sensenbrenner substitute was printed in the *Congressional Record* on July 16 and again on July 19. *See* 147 CONG.REC. H 4014-H4019 (daily ed. July 16, 2001) and H 4239-H 4243 (daily ed. July 19, 2001).

under charitable choice, (3) bar religious activity from taking place at the same time and place as a government funded program, (4) delete the provision allowing programs to be converted to vouchers if deemed "feasible and efficient" by the Secretary of the pertinent department, (5) eliminate the liability reform provisions regarding corporate contributions of equipment and supplies to charitable organizations, and (6) provide a revenue offset for the cost of the charitable giving tax incentives. Finally, the rule made in order one motion to recommit.[52]

(iii) House Floor Debate

After some delay because of concerns raised by a *Washington Post* article that disclosed an apparent agreement between the Salvation Army and the Administration concerning the issuance of a regulation to preempt state and local laws barring discrimination on the basis of sexual orientation in exchange for support for H.R. 7,[53] the House took up the measure on July 19, 2001, and adopted the rule, 228-199. After several hours of vigorous debate, the House then rejected the minority substitute described above, 168-231; rejected as well a motion to recommit offered by Rep. Conyers (D.-Mich.) incorporating the first two provisions of the rejected substitute which would have barred religious discrimination in employment as well as the preemption of state and local nondiscrimination statutes, 195-234; and adopted the bill, 233-198.[54] Prior to the vote on the minority substitute and in response to concerns raised during the debate about the preemption of state and local civil rights laws, Rep. Watts (R.-Ok.) made a commitment for himself and the other primary sponsor of H.R. 7, Rep. Hall (D.-Oh.) to "more clearly address this issue in conference."[55]

---

[52] The Rules Committee refused to allow three other amendments to be offered – one to bar religious groups receiving assistance from exempting themselves from state and local civil rights laws (defeated 4-9), another to prohibit direct funding of pervasively sectarian organizations (defeated 3-10), and a third to bar the tax provisions from taking effect if the Director of OMB projects a deficit outside of the Social Security and Medicare Trust Funds (defeated 3-10). *See id.* at 2.

[53] Dana Milbank, *Charity Cites Bush Help in Fight Against Hiring Gays*, Washington Post, July 10, 2001, at A1. Later that same day the White House Press Office issued a statement saying "The White House will not pursue the OMB regulation proposed by the Salvation Army and reported today."

[54] For the full debate on the bill, *see* 147 CONG.REC. H 4222 - H 4281 (daily ed. July 19, 2001). For the votes, *see id.* at H 42778-78, H 4280-81, and H 4281, respectively.

[55] *Id.* at H 4274 (statement of Mr. Watts of Oklahoma).

(iv) Senate Finance Committee Version

In the Senate H.R. 7 was referred to the Finance Committee. Because concerns about the civil rights and constitutional implications of the bill seemed to threaten its viability, Senators Lieberman (D.-Pa.) and Santorum (R.-Pa) initiated efforts to work out an acceptable compromise with the Administration. On February 8, 2002, they introduced the result of their efforts, S. 1924, the "CARE Act of 2002."[56] President Bush immediately endorsed the bill and urged its adoption.[57]

Like H.R. 7, S. 1924 contained tax incentives for charitable giving (albeit more generous ones) and modifications of the individual development account program. But it did not have H.R. 7's limitations on corporate liability nor most of its charitable choice provisions. With respect to the latter, Title III simply retained the provisions barring government at all levels from requiring religious organizations participating in publicly funded social services programs to remove religious art and icons from their premises or to change the religious elements of their names or charter documents; and it added a new prohibition barring government from requiring such organizations to change or remove religious requirements for membership on their governing boards. In addition, S. 1924

- mandated that nongovernmental organizations not be disadvantaged in applying to participate in federally funded social services programs simply because they had not previously participated (Title III);

- authorized social services grants or cooperative agreements to be awarded to intermediate organizations that could facilitate the participation of small nongovernmental providers (Title III)

- directed the IRS to adopt expedited procedures for acting on applications for tax-exempt status by social services providers (the EZ Pass system) (Title IV);

- authorized $150 million for a "Compassion Capital Fund" to enable several federal departments to provide technical and programmatic assistance to small community-based social services providers (Title V);

---

[56] 148 CONG. REC. S 546 (daily ed. February 8, 2002). The full title of the bill is the "Charity Aid, Recovery, and Empowerment Act of 2002."

[57] See n. 17.

- restored funding for the Social Services Block Grant program established under Title XX of the Social Security Act (Title VI); and

- authorized funding for a new program to support maternity group homes (Title VII).

S. 1924 was also referred to the Senate Finance Committee.

In two markup sessions in June on H.R. 7 and two tax bills, the Finance Committee incorporated a number of elements of S. 1924; and on July 16, 2002, it reported out its revised version of H.R. 7.[58] Also entitled the "CARE Act of 2002," the Committee's version of H.R. 7 contained a number of incentives for charitable giving, modified the individual development account program, restored funding for the Social Services Block Grant program, and included a variety of other tax initiatives. But it had none of the charitable choice provisions of the House-passed measure and none of the narrower counterpart provisions from Title III of S. 1924. It also did not have an authorization for a Compassion Capital Fund, as contemplated by Title V of S. 1924.

Subsequently, Senators Santorum and Lieberman led efforts to work out a unanimous consent agreement that would allow H.R. 7 to be taken up and several charitable choice-related proposals – including Titles III and V of S. 1924 as well as a proposal to bar subsidized providers from discriminating on religious grounds in their employment practices – to be offered as amendments. On October 14, 2002, Rep. Watts (R.-Ok.), one of the main House sponsors of H.R. 7 and a proponent of charitable choice, announced that he would accept the Santorum-Lieberman compromise if the Senate passed it; and that appeared to be the position of the Administration as well. But in the end no unanimous consent agreement could be worked out, and the 107th Congress came to an end without any further action on H.R. 7 or S. 1924.

(b) Re-authorization of Welfare Reform

As noted, the welfare reform measure that Congress enacted in 1996 was due for re-authorization in 2002. Charitable choice was part of that 1996 enactment and, consequently, the possibility existed that the 107th Congress might choose to revisit the issue in the course of revising and re-authorizing

---

[58] See S. Rept. 107-211 (July 16, 2002).

the program. Congress did not need to do so, because the existing charitable choice rules would continue to apply to the re-authorized program; but it could have. In the end Congress did not complete action on its re-authorization bills and deferred further action until after the 108th Congress convenes in January. But neither the bill passed by the House (H.R. 4737) or the one reported by the Senate Finance Committee evidenced any intent to revisit or modify the charitable choice provisions enacted in 1996.

The House-passed version of H.R. 4737 did contain two pertinent provisions. Section 103(b) would have authorized a new grant program to promote healthy marriages which would be subject to the existing charitable choice rules; and § 112(a)(1)(B) directed the states to include in their state plans a description of the "strategies and programs the State is undertaking" to implement the charitable choice provisions of the 1996 statute.

The version of H.R. 4737 reported by the Senate Finance Committee on July 25, 2002, also would have authorized a new grant program to promote healthy marriages (section 301) as well as a program of "Second Chance Homes" to help young mothers learn parenting skills in a group home setting (section 305). These programs, if enacted, would also have been subject to the existing charitable choice rules.[59]

In lieu of further action on these re-authorization measures, Congress included in the final continuing resolution for the session a provision extending the existing welfare program until January 11, 2003.[60]

(c) Other Measures

Another measure in the 107th Congress that once contained charitable choice provisions was S. 304, the "Drug Abuse Education, Prevention, and Treatment Act of 2001." As introduced on February 13, 2001, by Senators Hatch (R.-Ut.) and Leahy (D.-Vt.) and four co-sponsors, the bill would have extended charitable choice rules to a number of new programs, such as jail-based substance abuse programs, residential treatment programs for juveniles, programs to prevent delinquency through character education, and programs to help the children of prisoners. But in reporting the measure to the Senate on November 29, 2001, the Senate Judiciary Committee by voice vote approved a substitute measure that did not contain the charitable choice

---

[59] It might be noted that both measures would also have authorized a new program to promote fatherhood. But neither version of the program appears to have been made subject to charitable choice.
[60] P.L. 107-294 (Nov. 23, 2002).

provisions. (The committee did not issue a report.) The measure remained pending on the Senate calendar when Congress adjourned.

In addition, it might be noted that, as introduced, Title V of H.R. 1, the "No Child Left Behind Act of 2001," would have applied a charitable choice provision to drug and violence prevention programs and before- and after-school programs for school-age youth. But that provision was not included in the bill as reported[61] or as adopted by the House.[62] Nor was charitable choice part of the counterpart measure adopted by the Senate re-authorizing the Elementary and Secondary Education Act (S. 1, the "Better Education for Teachers and Students Act).[63] As a consequence, no charitable choice provisions were included in the measure as signed into law by President Bush on January 8, 2002 (although religious organizations are eligible to participate in providing after-school services authorized under the Act).[64]

(7) WHAT DID THE HOUSE-PASSED VERSION OF TITLE II OF H.R. 7 PROVIDE AND HOW DID IT DIFFER FROM PREVIOUS CHARITABLE CHOICE STATUTES?

The charitable choice title of H.R. 7, as approved by the Judiciary Committee and by the House, was a more elaborate version of what had previously been enacted and would not only have extended charitable choice to most of the federal government's social services programs but also allowed administrators to "voucherize" the programs if they deemed it "feasible and efficient" to do so. Title II contained a more expansive purposes section than prior enactments stating that the Act is intended not only to prohibit discrimination against religious organizations on the basis of their religious character and to protect the religious freedom of beneficiaries but also to provide assistance to individuals and families "in the most effective and efficient manner" and to facilitate the entry of religious and other community organizations in the administration and distribution of government assistance. In addition, with the provisions that differ from the previously enacted charitable choice statutes highlighted in italics, Title II of H.R. 7 would have:

---

[61] H. Rept. 107-63, Part I (May 14, 2001)).
[62] 147 CONG. REC. H 2421- H 2516 (daily ed. May 22, 2001).
[63] 147 CONG. REC. S 6305 (daily ed. June 14, 2001).
[64] P.L. 107-110 (January 8, 2002); 115 Stat. 1425.

(a) *extended charitable choice rules to federally funded activities in nine program areas – (1) the prevention and treatment of juvenile delinquency and the improvement of the juvenile justice system; (2) the prevention of crime and assistance to crime victims; (3) the provision of assistance under the federal housing statutes; (4) workforce investment under subtitles B or D of title I of the Workforce Investment Act of 1998[65]; (5) the Older Americans Act of 1965[66]; (6) intervention in and prevention of domestic violence; (7) hunger relief; (8) the Job Access and Reverse Commute grant program[67]; and (9) after-school and GED programs.*

(b) *stated that funds received by religious organizations are to be deemed aid to individuals and families and not to religion, and are not to be deemed "an endorsement by the government of religion or of the organization's religious beliefs or practices";*

(c) barred government from discriminating against religious organizations that seek to provide federally funded services because of their religious character;

(d) specified that a religious organization providing assistance "retain[s] its autonomy from Federal, State, and local governments";

(e) barred government from requiring religious organizations, as a condition of eligibility, to change their form of internal governance or to remove religious symbols or, *in new prohibitions, to change "provisions in [their] charter documents" or "to change [their] name[s]";*

(f) made clear that the Title VII exemption allowing religious organizations to discriminate on religious grounds in their employment practices is not affected by their receipt of federal funds;

(g) *provided that the Title VII exemption and the provisions of charitable choice generally override any contrary mandates in the programs to which charitable choice is extended by the bill;*

---

[65] 29 U.S.C.A. 2801 *et seq.*
[66] 42 U.S.C.A. 3001 *et seq.*
[67] 49 U.S.C.A. 5309 note.

(h) *stated explicitly that religious organizations receiving federal financial assistance pursuant to H.R. 7 must still comply with the nondiscrimination requirements of Title VI of the Civil Rights Act of 1964,*[68] *Title IX of the Education Amendments of 1972,*[69] *section 504 of the Rehabilitation Act of 1973,*[70] *and the Age Discrimination Act of 1975*[71];

(i) barred discrimination against beneficiaries generally "on the basis of religion, a religious belief, or a refusal to hold a religious belief" but, *in a new distinction, limited this nondiscrimination mandate only to admissions in programs funded by vouchers*;

(j) required that beneficiaries that object to the religious character of a provider be afforded an alternative provider of equal value which, *in modified language, is "unobjectionable to the individual on religious grounds"*;

(k) required that government ensure that notice is given to beneficiaries of their right to an alternative provider;

(l) required that the programs be implemented in a manner that is consistent with the establishment clause *and, as is also provided by one of the existing charitable choice statutes, the free exercise clause*;

(m) barred the use of funds provided directly (but not funds provided indirectly) to a religious organization for "sectarian instruction, worship, or proselytization";

(n) *required that religious activities offered by a religious organization receiving direct funding be "separate from the program funded under this subpart" and "voluntary for the individuals receiving services," and mandate that religious organizations certify that they will abide by these requirements*;

(o) *allowed assistance under all of the programs to which the charitable choice provisions of Title VII would apply to be distributed in the form of vouchers or certificates, if the Secretary of*

---

[68] 42 U.S.C.A. 2000d *et seq.* (barring discrimination on the bases of race, color, or national origin).
[69] 20 U.S.C.A. 1681 *et seq.* (barring discrimination on the basis of gender in federally assisted education programs).
[70] 29 U.S.C.A. 794 (barring discrimination on the basis of handicap).
[71] 42 U.S.C.A. 6101 *et seq.* (barring discrimination on the basis of age).

the administering department determines that to be "feasible and efficient";

(p) given the states a choice of commingling their own funds with the federal funds in the pertinent program or of keeping them separate but require that charitable choice rules apply to all commingled funds;

(q) required that religious organizations providing assistance be subject to the same regulations as other nongovernmental organizations and that their use of funds be subject to audit by the government, but allow, and in the case of direct assistance require, that public funds be kept in a separate account and that any audit be limited to that account;

(r) *required organizations providing services to conduct an annual self-audit;*

(s) *in a provision that was also in one of the drug abuse charitable choice statutes, imposed on nongovernmental entities that make subgrants the same charitable choice obligations imposed on government and, if such entities are religious in nature, extended to them the same rights otherwise afforded religious organizations*;

(t) allowed parties who believe their rights have been violated to bring suit in state and federal courts for injunctive relief, *but in contrast to existing charitable choice statutes, allowed suits only against the federal, state, or local governments and not against the service providers*; and

(u) *authorized $50 million to provide training and technical assistance to small nongovernmental organizations "in procedures relating to potential application and participation" in the pertinent programs, including assistance in setting up a 501(c)(3) organization, in applying for grants, and in complying with the federal nondiscrimination mandates.*

As noted, the version of H.R. 7 reported by the Senate Finance Committee on July 16, 2002, did not contain any of the foregoing provisions. (For a summary of the more modest provisions of S. 1924, see the preceding question.)

(8) WHAT IS THE LEGAL FRAMEWORK FOR THE CIVIL RIGHTS CONCERNS THAT HAVE BEEN RAISED ABOUT CHARITABLE CHOICE?

Several civil rights concerns have been raised in the debates on charitable choice. The primary one has been whether the religious exemption in Title VII of the Civil Rights Act of 1964, which allows religious organizations to discriminate on religious grounds in their employment practices, should apply to religious organizations that receive public funds under the rubric of charitable choice. There has also been some concern over the protections from discrimination afforded beneficiaries and, in an issue that has only become apparent in the debates on H.R. 7, on whether charitable choice should preempt state and local civil rights laws that go beyond federal nondiscrimination requirements and bar employment discrimination on such bases as sexual orientation and marital status.

These issues arise in the context of a complex panoply of civil rights mandates and exemptions that already exist. The following subsections explicate charitable choice with respect to (1) existing mandates barring discrimination in programs and activities that receive federal financial assistance, (2) existing mandates barring discrimination in employment practices, particularly Title VII of the Civil Rights Act of 1964 and its religious exemption, and (3) the preemption of state and local nondiscrimination laws that go beyond federal law. The question of the constitutionality of public aid going to organizations which discriminate on religious grounds in their employment practices is discussed in question 9.

(a) Nondiscrimination in Federally Assisted Programs

Federal law imposes a number of civil rights obligations on the provision of services in programs and activities that receive federal financial assistance:

- Title VI of the Civil Rights Act of 1964 bars discrimination on the bases of race, color, or national origin.[72]

---

[72] 42 U.S.C.A. 2000d *et seq.*

- Title IX of the Education Amendments of 1972 bars discrimination on the basis of sex and on the basis of blindness (in admissions) in education programs.[73]

- Section 504 of the Rehabilitation Act of 1973 bars discrimination on the basis of handicap.[74]

- The Age Discrimination Act of 1975 bars discrimination on the basis of age.[75]

All of these prohibitions on discrimination are triggered by the receipt of federal funds, but most of them apply only to the delivery of services and not to the employment practices of the entities that receive federal funds. The applicability of these statutes to federally financed programs and activities is not altered by charitable choice.[76]

In contrast, there is no comparable federal statute that generally bars **religious** discrimination in federally funded programs and activities. Individual programs sometimes contain such a prohibition,[77] but there is no general statutory prohibition.

Nonetheless, charitable choice has, since its inception as part of the welfare reform measure in 1996, included provisions that bar religious organizations from discriminating against beneficiaries on religious grounds and that require government to make an alternate provider available to any beneficiary who objects to the religious character of a given provider. But there have been some distinctions in the types of religious discrimination that are prohibited, and the House-passed version of H.R. 7 drew a new distinction based on whether the religious organization receives funding directly or indirectly. With respect to indirect assistance, H.R. 7 would have barred religious discrimination against individuals only in admissions.

All of the existing charitable choice statutes (as well as H.R. 7) bar a religious organization that receives assistance from discriminating against

---

[73] 20 U.S.C.A. 1681 *et seq.*
[74] 29 U.S.C.A. 794.
[75] 42 U.S.C.A. 6101 *et seq.*
[76] Because H.R. 7 contained a provision stating that any funds received under the rubric of charitable choice "constitute[] aid to individuals and families in need" and not aid to the organization, there was some concern in the House about whether Title VI, Title IX, Section 504, and the Age Discrimination Act would be applicable. Consequently, an amendment was agreed to in the committee markup and retained in the House-passed bill referencing these statutes and clarifying that "nothing in this section" affects their applicability.
[77] *See, e.g.*, the nondiscrimination prohibition attached to the Head Start program at 42 U.S.C.A. 9849(a).

beneficiaries on the basis of "religion" or "a religious belief." Three of the four statutes also bar such discrimination on the basis of a "refusal to actively participate in a religious practice." But H.R. 7 and one of the substance abuse statutes do not include this latter prohibition (although H.R. 7's requirement that participation in a religious activity must be voluntary is arguably equivalent). Moreover, H.R. 7 and the other drug abuse statute also bar discrimination on the basis of "a refusal to hold a religious belief." Finally, H.R. 7 as passed by the House would have applied its religious nondiscrimination mandates to all aspects of programs that are directly funded but only to admissions in programs that are indirectly funded. Given that H.R. 7 also would have allowed the Secretaries of the appropriate department to convert the programs to which the charitable choice provisions would be applied to vouchers if they find it to be "feasible and efficient," this distinction may have been significant.

(b) Nondiscrimination in Employment

Federal statutes impose a number of employment nondiscrimination requirements on public and private employers, and generally these are not dependent on whether or not the entity receives federal financial assistance, *i.e.*, they are regulatory requirements that apply regardless of whether an entity receives federal assistance. With the exception of Title IX, none of the nondiscrimination statutes described in the previous subsection applies to the employment practices of entities that receive federal funds (unless a primary objective of the federally funded program is to provide employment). But most public and private employers that employ more than a specified number of employees are barred by the Americans with Disabilities Act from discriminating in their employment practices on the basis of disability,[78] by the Age Discrimination in Employment Act on the basis of age,[79] and by Title VII of the Civil Rights Act of 1964 on the bases of race, color, national origin, sex, and religion.[80]

A number of these statutes contain special provisions with respect to the employment practices of religious institutions. Religious educational institutions are exempt from the sex nondiscrimination requirement of Title IX, for instance, if "the application of this subsection would not be consistent

---

[78] 42 U.S.C.A. 12201 *et seq.*
[79] 29 U.S.C.A. 621 *et seq.*
[80] 42 U.S.C.A. 2000e *et seq.*

with the religious tenets of such organization."[81] The Americans with Disabilities Act, while barring religious organizations from discriminating on the basis of disability in employment, specifically provides that they may still give preference in their employment practices on the basis of religion and may require their employees to conform to their religious tenets.[82] Most important, Title VII specifically exempts religious employers from its ban on religious discrimination in employment.

Title VII and the Religious Exemption

It is the Title VII exemption that has generated extensive debate in the discussion of charitable choice, because all of the charitable choice statutes and proposals so far, including the House-passed version of H.R. 7, have explicitly provided that the Title VII exemption "shall not be affected by the religious organization's provision of assistance under, or receipt of funds from, a program described in ...."[83] (Neither the Senate Finance Committee version of H.R. 7 nor S. 1924, it should be noted, contained such a provision.)

Title VII bars most public and private employers with 15 or more employees from discriminating in their employment practices on the bases of race, color, national origin, sex, and religion. This threshold requirement of 15 employees means that many churches, synagogues, and other congregational entities, as well as small religious social services providers, are not large enough to be covered by any of the nondiscrimination mandates of Title VII. But Section 702 of Title VII specifically exempts those religious employers that are large enough to be covered from its prohibition on religious discrimination, as follows:

> This title shall not apply ... to a religious corporation, association, educational institution, or society with respect to the employment of individuals of a particular religion to perform work connected with the

---

[81] 20 U.S.C.A. 1681(a)(3).
[82] 42 U.S.C.A. 12113(c).
[83] Title II of H.R. 7 as introduced included as well a provision that would have allowed religious entities receiving public funds to require their employees to adhere to their "religious practices." Given the broad construction that has been given the Title VII exemption, that provision likely added nothing to the Title VII exemption. But in any event, the provision was not part of the manager's substitute for Title II proposed at the beginning of the markup of H.R. 7 by the House Judiciary Committee and was not part of the bill as approved by the committee or by the House.

carrying on by such corporation, association, educational institution, or society of its activities.[84]

Thus, religious organizations otherwise covered by Title VII may use religion as a criterion in their hiring, firing, promotion, and other employment practices; and they may do so not only with respect to employees engaged in religious activities but also those engaged in purely secular activities. This exemption has been unanimously upheld as constitutional by the Supreme Court with respect to the nonprofit activities of religious organizations[85] and has been applied to allow a wide variety of religious entities to discriminate on religious grounds in a wide variety of circumstances.[86]

---

[84] 42 U.S.C.A. 2000e-1. Title VII also contains two other exemptions, now largely redundant, allowing religious employers to discriminate on religious grounds. The first allows educational institutions that are religiously controlled or that are "directed toward the propagation of a particular religion" to discriminate on religious grounds in their employment practices. The second allows all employers, not just religious organizations, to use religion, sex, or national origin as a criterion in their employment practices if religion, sex, or national origin "is a bona fide occupational qualification reasonably necessary to the normal operation of that particular business or enterprise." See 42 U.S.C.A. 2000e-2(e).

[85] Corporation of the Presiding Bishop of Church of Jesus Christ of Latter-Day Saints v. Amos, 483 U.S. 327 (1987). The Court offered no comment with respect to the constitutionality of the exemption as it might be applied to any profit-making activities of religious organizations.

[86] See, e.g., Corporation of the Presiding Bishop v. Amos, *supra* (church fired a building engineer employed in a church-owned gymnasium open to the public because he failed to qualify for a "temple recommend"); Little v. Wuerl, 929 F.2d 944 (3d Cir. 1991) (Catholic school fired a teacher who had remarried without first seeking an annulment of her first marriage in accord with Catholic doctrine); Porth v. Roman Catholic Diocese of Kalamazoo, 209 Mich.App. 630, 532 N.W.2d 195 (Mich. App. 1995) (Catholic school refused to renew the contract of a Protestant teacher after it had decided to hire only Catholics as faculty members); Walker v. First Orthodox Presbyterian Church, 22 FEP Cases 761 (Cal. 1980) (church fired its organist on the grounds his homosexuality conflicted with the church's beliefs); Boyd v. Harding Academy of Memphis, Inc., 88 F.3d 410 (6th Cir. 1996) (Christian school fired an unmarried female teacher after she became pregnant because of its beliefs opposing extramarital sex); Maguire v. Marquette University, 814 F.2d 1213 (7th Cir. 1987) (Catholic university refused to hire a female professor because her views on abortion were not in accord with Catholic doctrine); EEOC v. Presbyterian Ministries, Inc., 788 F.Supp. 1154 (W.D. Wash. 1992) (a Christian retirement home fired a Muslim receptionist because she insisted on wearing a head covering as required by her faith); Piatti v. Jewish Community Centers of Greater Boston, Mass. LEXIS 733 (1993) (a Jewish community center refused to hire a Catholic as a youth director); Feldstein v. Christian Science Monitor, 555 F.Supp. 974 (D. Mass. 1983) (a newspaper owned by the Christian Scientist Church refused to hire applicants of other faiths); and Hall v. Baptist Memorial Health Care Corporation, 215 F.3d 618 (6th Cir. 2000) (a Baptist health care corporation fired an employee because she had assumed a leadership role in a church that welcomed and supported gay and lesbian individuals).

As noted, Title VII is a regulatory statute. Nothing in its language generally or in the religious exemption provision (§ 702) suggests that either is limited to situations in which an employer does not receive public funds. The case in which the Supreme Court upheld § 702 as constitutional did not involve any public funding,[87] but several lower federal courts have held the exemption to be applicable to religious organizations receiving public funds.[88] Nonetheless, apparently to eliminate any possible misunderstanding, all four charitable choice statutes as well as Title II of H.R. 7 state explicitly that the religious exemption in Title VII is not lost simply because a religious employer receives public funds.

Religious organizations that meet the minimum size requirement of Title VII (*i.e.* 15 or more employees) are **not** exempt from the other employment nondiscrimination requirements of Title VII regarding race, color, national origin, and sex; and charitable choice does not alter, or propose to alter, the applicability of these requirements. Thus, religious organizations have in a number of instances been held liable under Title VII for discrimination on the bases of race, sex, or national origin.[89] It can sometimes be a close question, however, whether the alleged discrimination by a religious employer is based on religion or one of the prohibited bases of discrimination.[90]

---

[87] Corporation of the Presiding Bishop of the Church of Jesus Christ of Latter-Day Saints, *supra*, n. 6.

[88] *See, e.g.*, Hall v. Baptist Memorial Health Care Corporation, supra, n. 10 (student assistance); Siegel v. Truett-McConnell College, supra, n. 11 (student assistance); Young v. Shawnee Mission Medical Center, Civ. No. 88-2321-S (D. Kan., decided Oct. 21, 1988) (Medicare payments); Dodge v. Salvation Army, 1989 U.S.Dist.LEXIS 4797, 48 Empl. Prac. Dec. (CCH) P38,619 (S.D. Miss. 1989) (unspecified public funding of a Victims Assistance Coordinator position).

[89] *See, e.g.*, EEOC v. Pacific Press Publishing House, 676 F.2d 1272 (9th Cir. 1982) (publishing house had fired a female employee after she complained that she had been denied monetary allowances paid to similarly situation male employees); EEOC v. Lutheran Family Services in the Carolinas, 884 F.Supp. 1033 (E.D. N.C. 1994) (a religious social services provider had refused to give a pregnant employee a leave of absence but gave extended leaves of absence to male employees for a variety of reasons); and EEOC v. Southwestern Baptist Theological Seminary, 651 F.2d 277 (5th Cir. 1981), *cert. den.*, 456 U.S. 905 (1982) (seminary held to be subject to filing information reports on its employment practices with respect to staff in its non-academic departments).

[90] In several cases the courts have refused to grant summary judgment in favor of Christian schools that had each fired an unmarried female teacher who had become pregnant, saying that if the dismissals were due to the teachers' adultery the Title VII religious exemption would apply but that dismissal for pregnancy alone would constitute forbidden sex discrimination. *See* Vigars v. Valley Christian Center of Dublin, Cal., 805 F.Supp. 802 (N.D. Cal. 1992); Ganzy v. Allen Christian School, 995 F.Supp. 340 (E.D. N.Y. 1998); and Cline v. Catholic Diocese of Toledo, 199 F.3d 853 (6th Cir. 1999).

Ministerial Exception

It should be noted that the Title VII exemption overlaps to some degree with a constitutionally-based employment discrimination exemption for religious organizations that has been labeled the "ministerial exception." This exception exempts religious organizations from **all** statutory prohibitions on discrimination with respect to the employment of ministers and other ecclesiastical personnel. The free exercise of religion clause of the First Amendment, it has been held, bars the government from interfering in any way with the relationship between a religious institution and its ministers. The ministerial exception has been held to apply to the employment of ministers (including youth ministers, probationary ministers, and ministers of music), seminary faculty, and hospital chaplains.[91] It has been held **not** to apply, however, with respect to the employment by religious organizations of persons who are not engaged in a religious ministry or in the training of persons for such ministries, such as the administrative and support staff in religious institutions.[92] Because the ministerial exemption is constitutionally based, it is not modified by charitable choice in any way.

Thus, under the Title VII exemption a religious organization can discriminate on religious grounds with respect to all of its employees; but if it meets the minimum size requirement, it is otherwise subject to the statute's employment nondiscrimination mandates. With respect to the employment of its spiritual leaders, however, a religious organization, pursuant to the ministerial exception, is unconstrained by **any** nondiscrimination requirement

---

[91] *See* McClure v. Salvation Army, 460 F.2d 553 (5th Cir.), *cert. den.*, 409 U.S. 896 (1972) (firing of a female officer in the Salvation Army after she claimed she was given a lower salary and fewer benefits than male officers held to be within the scope of the ministerial exemption); Bryce v. Episcopal Church in the Diocese of Colorado, 121 F.Supp.2d 1327 (firing of youth minister by her church after she participated in a commitment ceremony with her partner held to be a constitutionally exempt act); Young v. Northern Illinois Conference of the United Methodist Church, 21 F.3d 184 (7th Cir. 1994), *cert. den.*, 513 U.S. 929 (1994) (conference of churches' refusal to change the probationary status of an African-American minister held to be constitutionally exempt);EEOC v. The Roman Catholic Diocese of Raleigh, N.C., 213 F.3d 795 (4th Cir.), *cert. den.*, 69 U.S.L.W. 3206 (2000) (church fired its minister of music);EEOC v. Southwestern Baptist Theological Seminary, *supra* (seminary's criteria for its faculty held to be constitutionally exempt from monitoring and examination by the EEOC); and Sharon v. St. Luke's Presbyterian School of Theology, 713 N.E.2d 334 (Ind. Ct. App., 1st Dist., 1999) (firing of a chaplain by a religiously affiliated hospital held to be constitutionally protected).

[92] *See, e.g.*, EEOC v. Southwestern Baptist Theological Seminary, *supra* (administrative and support staff in a seminary) and EEOC v. Pacific Press Publishing Association, 676 F.2d 1272 (9th Cir. 1982) (editorial support staff in a religious publishing house).

(c) Preemption of State and Local Civil Rights Laws

An issue that received only slight attention in previous debates on charitable choice gained substantial visibility during House consideration of H.R. 7. That issue concerns the preemptive effect of charitable choice on state and local civil rights laws that bar forms of discrimination that are not barred by federal law, such as discrimination based on sexual orientation or marital status. All of the charitable choice statutes that have been enacted, as well as Title II of H.R. 7, provide that a religious organization that is a program participant "shall retain its independence from Federal, State, and local government, including such organization's control over the definition, development, practice, and expression of its religious beliefs." But prior to the House debate on H.R. 7, there had been no legislative history explicating the meaning of this provision. Similarly, all of the charitable choice statutes and proposals have barred government from requiring that a religious provider "alter its form of internal governance" and, as noted above, have explicitly provided that a religious organization's exemption under Title VII "shall not be affected by its participation in, or receipt of funds from, a designated program." But with the exception of a provision added to the charitable choice statute concerning substance abuse programs,[93] little attention has been paid to whether these provisions might have a preemptive effect on state and local civil rights laws.

The House debate on H.R. 7 made clear that these provisions, and particularly the first one concerning the independence of religious organizations, are intended to preempt state and local civil rights laws. The report of the House Judiciary Committee stated:

> Because H.R. 7 expands charitable choice principles to cover many new Federal programs, one uniform rule should apply to all programs and allow religious organizations to retain their autonomy over the definition, development, practice, and expression of their religious beliefs, including through hiring staff. This is so even when State or local laws provide otherwise .... Wherever federal funds go, this statutory right of religious organizations to staff on a religious basis should follow ....[94]

---

[93] P.L. 106-554,which added charitable choice provisions to Title V of the Public Health Services Act, prefaced the Title VII exemption language with the following sentence: "Nothing in this section shall be construed to modify or affect the provisions of any other Federal or State law or regulation that relates to discrimination in employment."

[94] H. Rept. 107-138, Part I, *supra*, at 37.

The report similarly made clear that if state and local funds are commingled with federal funds in an applicable program, state and local civil rights laws will not apply to those funds.[95]

Under the supremacy clause of the Constitution,[96] it seems clear that Congress has the power to preempt state and local laws pursuant to charitable choice. What has been the subject of debate has been the desirability of doing so in this case.

(9) DOES CHARITABLE CHOICE VIOLATE THE ESTABLISHMENT OF RELIGION CLAUSE OF THE FIRST AMENDMENT?

As noted in question 1, the charitable choice statutes and Title II of H.R. 7 contain a number of provisions that seem intended to ensure their constitutionality. All of these measures require that they be implemented "consistent with the Establishment Clause of the United States Constitution." All require that public funds that are disbursed directly to religious organizations not be used for purposes of religious worship, instruction, or proselytization. All have provisions to protect those who receive services from religious organizations from religious discrimination. All require equal treatment, but not preferential treatment, for religious organizations seeking to participate in government social services programs. Title II of H.R. 7, although not the charitable choice statutes previously enacted into law, also would have required that any religious activity offered by a religious organization be separate from the program that receives direct federal assistance and that participation in any religious activity that is directly funded be voluntary for the individuals receiving services.

---

[95] *Id.* at 38. During the markup of the bill, Rep. Sensenbrenner responded to a question from Rep. Frank about the preemptive effect of the measure on state and local laws by stating that "Federal law applies where Federal funds go, and State law does not apply." *Id.* at 176. The committee also rejected an amendment by Rep. Frank to bar religious organizations receiving assistance from discriminating against any individual "on any basis prohibited under applicable Federal, State, or local law ...." *Id.* at 249-254. It rejected as well an amendment by Rep. Jackson-Lee specifying that religious organizations receiving assistance would not be exempt from state and local laws. *Id.* at 258-266. Floor debate during House consideration of H.R. 7 also made clear the preemptive effect of the bill on state and local laws.

[96] U.S. Constitution, Art. VI, cl. 2: "This Constitution, and the Laws of the United States which shall be made in Pursuance thereof ... shall be the supreme Law of the Land."

On the other hand, all of the statutes as well as H.R. 7 also allow religious organizations that receive public funds to discriminate on religious grounds with respect to their employees, to display religious symbols on the premises where services are provided, and to practice and express their religious beliefs independent of any government restrictions. None of them, moreover, require the publicly funded program to be separately incorporated from its sponsoring religious organization. In addition, the measures allow religious organizations that receive public funds indirectly, *i.e.,* by means of vouchers, to engage in religious worship, instruction, and proselytization in the funded program and to impose religious requirements on beneficiaries after they are once admitted to a program. Finally, all of the charitable choice initiatives seem premised on the assumption that charitable choice will in some manner allow religious organizations to employ their faiths in carrying out the publicly funded programs, regardless of whether they are directly or indirectly funded.

As a consequence, questions have been raised about whether charitable choice on its face or in its implementation is consistent with the establishment of religion clause of the First Amendment. One aspect of this issue concerns whether it is constitutional for public funds to go to organizations that discriminate on religious grounds in their employment practices. More generally, the question is whether it is constitutional for public funds to go to religious organizations that have the characteristics detailed in the previous paragraph and that in some manner employ their faiths in carrying out the funded programs.

These questions of constitutionality, in turn, have at least two dimensions. The charitable choice statutes and proposals govern public aid that is given **directly** to religious organizations by means of grants or cooperative agreements in the specified programs and, at least in the cases of TANF and Title II of H.R. 7, public aid that is given **indirectly** in the form of vouchers that can be redeemed with religious (as well as nonreligious) organizations. The constitutional strictures that apply to these two forms of aid differ; and as a consequence, the form in which the public aid is provided to religious organizations under charitable choice has implications for the constitutionality of the aid.

These questions are further complicated by the fact that the Supreme Court's interpretation of the establishment clause has been shifting. Prior to its recent decisions, the Court's construction of the establishment clause made it difficult, if not impossible, for religious organizations that are deemed pervasively sectarian to receive aid directly from the government, even for avowedly secular purposes, and have required that programs receiving direct public aid be essentially secular in nature. But the Court's recent decisions in *Agostini v. Felton*[97] and *Mitchell v. Helms*[98] have relaxed the strictures on direct aid and eliminated the pervasively sectarian barrier, although the Court still requires that direct aid to religious institutions not be used for religious indoctrination. With respect to indirect assistance, the Court's past jurisprudence has been less restrictive; and its recent decision in *Zelman v. Simmons-Harris*[99] appears to legitimate an even broader array of voucher programs.

The following subsections detail the constitutional frameworks that appear to govern direct and indirect aid and apply them to H.R. 7:

(a) Direct Aid

In general terms the establishment clause has been construed by the Supreme Court to "absolutely prohibit government-financed or government-sponsored indoctrination into the beliefs of a particular religious faith."[100] "[G]overnment inculcation of religious beliefs," the Court has stated, "has the impermissible effect of advancing religion."[101] To guard against that effect, public assistance which flows **directly** to religious institutions in the form of grants or cooperative agreements has been required by the Court to be limited to aid that is "secular, neutral, and nonideological...."[102] Government has been able to provide direct support to **secular** programs and services sponsored or provided by religious entities, but it has been barred from directly subsidizing such organizations' religious activities or proselytizing.[103]

The Court gradually distilled the constitutional requirements governing direct aid into a tripartite test. That test, known as the *Lemon* test after the case in which it was first given full expression, required public aid to meet all of the following requirements:

> First, the statute must have a secular legislative purpose; second, its principal or primary effect must be one that neither advances nor inhibits

---

[97] 521 U.S. 203 (1997).
[98] 530 U.S. 793 (2000).
[99] 122 S.Ct. 2460 (2002).
[100] Grand Rapids School District v. Ball, 473 U.S. 373, 385 (1973).
[101] Agostini v. Felton, 521 U.S. 203, 223 (1997).
[102] Committee for Public Education v. Nyquist, 413 U.S. 756, 780 (1973).
[103] Committee for Public Education v. Nyquist, *supra*; Lemon v. Kurtzman, 403 U.S. 602 (1971); Bowen v. Kendrick, 487 U.S. 589 (1988).

religion ...; finally, the statute must not foster "an excessive entanglement with religion."[104]

The secular purpose prong has rarely posed a serious obstacle to the constitutionality of a direct aid program, but the Court's original formulations of the primary effect and entanglement tests often proved fatal to programs providing direct aid to pervasively religious institutions. The Court construed the primary effect test to mean that direct public aid must be limited to secular use. Thus, a direct aid program could founder on this aspect of the *Lemon* test in either of two ways. It could be held unconstitutional if the aid was not limited to secular use either by its nature or by statutory or regulatory constraint.[105] It could also be held unconstitutional if it flowed to institutions that the Court deemed to be pervasively sectarian, *i.e.*, entities whose religious and secular functions were so "inextricably intertwined" that its secular functions could not be isolated for purposes of public aid.[106]

Moreover, even if an aid program was limited to secular use, it often foundered on the excessive entanglement prong of the *Lemon* test. Particularly in the context of direct aid to pervasively sectarian organizations, the Court held that government had to closely monitor the use religious organizations made of the aid provided in order to be sure that the limitation to secular use was observed. But the very act of monitoring, the Court sometimes said, excessively intruded the government into the affairs of the religious institution; and for that reason the aid program was unconstitutional.[107]

Thus, under this application of the *Lemon* test, religious organizations were not automatically disqualified from participating in public programs providing direct assistance. But in order to meet the secular use requirement, such organizations had either to divest themselves of their religious character and to become predominantly secular in nature or, at the least, to be able to separate their secular functions and activities from their religious functions and activities. To the extent they did so, it was deemed constitutionally permissible for government to provide direct funding to their secular functions. This former interpretation of the establishment clause also

---

[104] Lemon v. Kurtzman, 403 U.S. 602, 612-13 (1971).
[105] *See, e.g.*, Committee for Public Education v. Nyquist, *supra*; Meek v. Pittenger, 421 U.S. 349 (1975); Wolman v. Walter, 433 U.S. 229 (1977).
[106] *See, e.g.*, Wolman v. Walter, *supra*, and School District of the City of Grand Rapids v. Ball, 473 U.S. 373 (1985).
[107] Lemon v. Kurtzman, *supra*; Meek v. Pittenger, *supra*; Aguilar v. Felton, 473 U.S. 402 (1985).

generally meant that it was constitutionally **impermissible** for religious organizations that are **pervasively sectarian** to participate in direct public aid programs.[108]

As a practical matter, these interpretations of the establishment clause had their most severe effects on programs providing direct aid to sectarian elementary and secondary schools, because the Court presumed that such schools are pervasively sectarian. The Court presumed to the contrary with respect to sectarian colleges, hospitals, and other social welfare organizations, although it held open the possibility that some of these agencies might be pervasively sectarian.[109]

In its most recent decisions, however, the Court has reformulated the *Lemon* test and abandoned the presumption that some religious institutions, such as sectarian elementary and secondary schools, are so pervasively sectarian that they are constitutionally ineligible to participate in direct public aid programs. The Court still requires that direct public aid serve a secular purpose, not have a primary effect of advancing or inhibiting religion, and not lead to excessive entanglement. But the primary effect test now means that the aid itself must be secular in nature; it must be distributed on a religiously neutral basis; and it must not be used for purposes of religious indoctrination. Moreover, the Court has now made the excessive entanglement test one aspect of the primary effect inquiry; and it no longer

---

[108] The Court did not lay down a hard and fast definition of what makes an organization pervasively sectarian. But it looked at such factors as the proximity of the organization in question to a sponsoring church; the presence of religious symbols and paintings on the premises; formal church or denominational control over the organization; whether a religious criterion is applied in the hiring of employees or in the selection of trustees or, in the case of a school, to the admission of students; statements in the organization's charter or other publications that its purpose is the propagation and promotion of religious faith; whether the organization engages in religious services or other religious activities; its devotion, in the case of schools, to academic freedom; *etc. See, e.g.*, Bradfield v. Roberts, 175 U.S. 291 (1899); Lemon v. Kurtzman, *supra*; Tilton v. Richardson, 403 U.S. 672 (1971); Committee for Public Education v. Nyquist, *supra*; Meek v. Pittenger, 421 U.S. 349 (1975); Roemer v. Maryland Board of Public Works, 426 U.S. 736 (1976); and Bowen v. Kendrick, 487 U.S. 589 (1988). But the Court has also made clear that "it is not enough to show that the recipient of a ... grant is affiliated with a religious institution or that it is 'religiously inspired.'" Bowen v. Kendrick, *supra*, at 621. Indeed, none of these factors, by itself, has been held sufficient to make an institution pervasively sectarian and therefore ineligible for direct aid. Such a finding has always rested on a combination of factors. For useful lower federal court discussions of the criteria bearing on whether an institution is pervasively sectarian or not, *see* Minnesota Federation of Teachers v. Nelson, 740 F.Supp. 694 (D. Minn. 1990) and Columbia Union College v. Clark, 159 F.3d 151 (4th Cir. 1998), *cert. denied*, 527 U.S. 1013 (1999), *on remand sub nom* Columbia Union College v. Oliver, 2000 U.S.Dist.LEXIS 13644 (D. Md. 2000), *aff'd*, 2001 U.S.App.LEXIS 14253 (4th Cir. decided June 26, 2001).

[109] *See* Bowen v. Kendrick, 487 U.S. 589 (1988).

assumes that such entanglement is the inevitable result of government oversight of its aid program.

Three years ago in *Agostini v. Felton*[110] the Court for the first time overturned a prior establishment clause decision and held it to be constitutional for public school teachers to provide remedial and enrichment services on the premises of private sectarian schools to children attending those schools who were eligible for such services under Title I of the Elementary and Secondary Education Act.[111] The earlier decision of *Aguilar v. Felton, supra*, had found the delivery of such services on the premises of sectarian elementary and secondary schools to be excessively entangling, because the pervasively sectarian nature of the institutions required government to engage in a very intrusive monitoring to be sure that the Title I employees did not inculcate religion. But in *Agostini* the Court stated that subsequent decisions had abandoned the presumption that "public employees will inculcate religion simply because they happen to be in a sectarian environment."[112] As a consequence, it said, .it had also to "discard the assumption that *pervasive* monitoring of Title I teachers is required."[113] The Court also stated that

> the factors we use to assess whether an entanglement is "excessive" are similar to the factors we use to examine "effect" .... Thus, it is simplest to recognize why entanglement is significant and treat it ... as an aspect of the inquiry into a statute's effect.[114]

Most recently, the Court in *Mitchell v. Helms*[115] upheld as constitutional an ESEA program which subsidizes the acquisition and use of educational materials and equipment by public and private schools. More particularly, the Court found the provision of such items as computer hardware and software, library books, movie projectors, television sets, tape recorders, VCRs, laboratory equipment, maps, and cassette recordings to private sectarian elementary and secondary schools not to violate the establishment clause. In the process the Court overturned parts of two prior decisions which had held similar aid programs to be unconstitutional and which had been premised on the view that direct aid to pervasively sectarian institutions

---

[110] 521 U.S. 203 (1997).
[111] The Agostini decision overturned in its entirety the Court's decision in Aguilar v. Felton, 473 U.S. 402 (1985) but also overturned parts of Meek v. Pittenger, *supra*, and City of Grand Rapids v. Ball, 473 U.S. 373 (1985).
[112] Agostini v. Felton, *supra*, at 234.
[113] *Id.*
[114] *Id.* at 232-33.

is constitutionally suspect.[116] Although the Justices could not agree on a majority opinion, the plurality opinion by Justice Thomas and the concurring opinion by Justice O'Connor (joined by Justice Breyer) both appear to have eliminated pervasive sectarianism as a constitutionally preclusive characteristic regarding direct aid and modified the primary effect test accordingly. *Agostini* had hinted at this result but *Mitchell* confirmed it. As summarized by Justice O'Connor, the primary effect test now has three essential elements:

> (1) whether the aid results in governmental indoctrination, (2) whether the aid program defines its recipients by reference to religion, and (3) whether the aid creates an excessive entanglement between government and religion.[117]

Thus, the Court now appears to construe the establishment clause to allow some forms of direct aid to religious entities that formerly were deemed constitutionally excluded because of their pervasively religious character. Under the reformulated *Lemon* test, direct public aid must still serve a secular purpose and not create an excessive entanglement. But the most critical elements appear to be that the aid is distributed in a religiously neutral manner, *i.e.*, that it does not define its recipients on the basis of religion and provide an incentive for beneficiaries to undertake religious indoctrination, and that it does not result in religious indoctrination which is attributable to the government.

(b) Indirect Aid

Indirect aid in the form of tax benefits or vouchers, however, was less constrained prior to the Court's recent revisions of its establishment clause jurisprudence; and the Court's most recent decision in *Zelman v. Simmons-Harris*[118] appears to loosen the constitutional bounds even more. Like its standards for direct aid, the Court requires that indirect aid programs serve a secular purpose and be distributed to their initial beneficiaries on a religiously neutral basis, *i.e.*, that the beneficiaries not be chosen or given preference on the basis of a religious criterion. But the critical element seems

---

[115] 530 U.S. 793 (2000).
[116] Overturned in part were Meek v. Pittenger, 421 U.S. 349 (1975) and Wolman v. Walter, 433 U.S. 229 (1977).
[117] Mitchell v. Helms, *supra*, at 845 (opinion of O'Connor, J.).
[118] 122 S.Ct. 2460 (2002).

to be whether the initial beneficiaries have a "true private choice" in deciding whether to obtain subsidized services from secular or religious providers.

In its earlier decisions the Court held indirect aid programs unconstitutional if they had been designed in such a manner that the universe of choice available to the beneficiaries was almost entirely religious.[119] But if the initial beneficiaries had a genuinely independent choice among secular and religious providers, the Court held the programs constitutional and ruled that even pervasively sectarian entities were not precluded from participating.[120] Indeed, the Court made clear that indirect aid which ultimately is channeled to religious institutions does not have to be restricted to secular use but can be used for all of the institutions' functions, including their religious ones.[121]

The Court's recent decision in *Zelman v. Simmons-Harris, supra,* further loosened the constitutional constraints on indirect aid. That case involved a program of educational vouchers that low-income parents could use at private schools in the city of Cleveland. Most of those schools were religious in nature. But the Court held that in evaluating whether the parents had a true private choice in using the aid, **all** of the educational options open to the parents needed to be considered and not just the private school options. Thus, enrollment in public schools, magnet schools, and community schools, as well as the possibility of receiving special tutoring assistance, all needed to be considered as options along with the private religious and secular school possibilities. In other words, the Court held that the universe of choice available to the voucher recipients was not defined solely by the private providers where the vouchers could be used but included a number of public school and non-voucher educational options as well.

(c) Constitutionality of Charitable Choice

Some aspects of the charitable choice proposals that have been enacted as well as Title II of H.R. 7 likely satisfy the foregoing requirements. That

---

[119] Committee for Public Education v. Nyquist, *supra,* and Sloan v. Lemon, *supra*.

[120] Mueller v. Allen, 463 US. 388 (1983); Witters v. Washington Department of Social Services, 474 U.S. 481 (1986); Zobrest v. Catalina Foothills School District, 509 U.S. 1 (1993); Zelman v. Simmons-Harris, *supra*.

[121] For a more detailed examination of the constitutional standards governing indirect aid, including the Court's decision in Zelman v. Simmons-Harris, *supra,* and for summaries of recent state and lower federal court decisions, see CRS Report RL30165, *Education Vouchers: Constitutional Issues and Cases*.

seems particularly to be the case with respect to social services aid that is provided in the form of vouchers. The Court's interpretations of the establishment clause make clear that such aid can ultimately flow even to pervasively sectarian institutions, so long as the initial recipients have a true private choice among service providers. That means both that such aid can go to religious entities that discriminate on religious grounds in their employment practices[122] and that such entities need not be barred from engaging in religious worship, instruction, and proselytizing in programs receiving such support. Thus, there does not appear to be a constitutional problem in the provisions of the charitable choice statutes as well as H.R. 7 that allow such employment discrimination and that permit religious institutions receiving social services aid indirectly to engage in religious worship, instruction, or proselytizing in the subsidized program.

Nonetheless, there may still be a constitutional question raised about charitable choice with respect to indirect aid. The critical issue for indirect aid continues to be whether there is a genuinely independent decision-maker between the government and the entity that ultimately receives the assistance or whether the government has dictated that the aid ultimately goes to a religious entity. All of the charitable choice measures require that those who object to a particular religious provider be given an alternative that is either secular or, as in H.R. 7, not religiously objectionable. But they do not require that a voucher recipient have a choice of secular and religious providers initially. Whether this is sufficient to meet the Court's standards does not seem certain.

Whether **direct** aid to religious entities that discriminate on religious grounds in their employment practices, as allowed by all of the charitable choice statutes as well as the House-passed version of H.R. 7, can pass constitutional muster seems more complex but still likely. Prior to *Mitchell*

---

[122] A number of recent lower court decisions have held that religious colleges and hospitals do not forfeit their Title VII exemption as a result of receiving public funds indirectly in the form of student aid and Medicare payments. *See, e.g.,* Young v. Shawnee Mission Medical Center, 1988 U.S.Dist.LEXIS 12248 (D. Kan. 1988) (court held that the Title VII exemption applied to a religiously affiliated hospital's firing of a clerk-receptionist because she was not a Seventh Day Adventist, notwithstanding the hospital's acceptance of Medicare payments); Siegel v. Truett-McConnell College, Inc., 13 F.Supp.2d 1335 (N.D. Ga. 1994) (Baptist college's firing of a teacher because he was not a Christian held to be protected by Title VII notwithstanding college's receipt of public funds from a federal student assistance program); and Hall v. Baptist Memorial Health Care Corporation, 215 F.23d 618 (6th Cir. 2000) (Baptist college's firing of a student services specialist because she had become a lay minister in a community church that welcomed gay and lesbian members held to be protected by Title VII exemption notwithstanding the college's receipt of public funds by means of unspecified federal student assistance programs).

the Court's decisions had often used such employment discrimination as an indicator that an entity was pervasively sectarian and, hence, ineligible for direct assistance.[123] But it had never relied on that factor alone; other factors always entered into the constitutional equation.[124]

Those rulings, consequently, seem to suggest that religious discrimination in employment, by itself, might not have been enough to render a direct aid program unconstitutional. *Mitchell* seems to strengthen that possibility, at least for certain kinds of direct aid. In that case, as noted, the Court upheld as constitutional a direct aid program providing educational supplies and equipment to entities that the Court had previously found to be pervasively sectarian and had previously held to be constitutionally barred from receiving such aid – sectarian elementary and secondary schools. In so doing the Court shifted the constitutional focus from the nature of the organization receiving the aid to whether the aid is distributed in a religiously neutral manner and whether it is used for religious indoctrination. As a consequence, whether the entity receiving the assistance discriminates on religious grounds in its employment practices seems to have become of little or no concern, at least for inkind direct assistance.

The more critical question concerns the role of faith in carrying out social services programs that are directly subsidized. The Court's decisions make clear that direct public aid cannot be used for religious indoctrination, and all of the charitable choice measures as well as the House-passed version of H.R. 7 seem to meet this requirement by explicitly prohibiting direct aid from being used for religious worship, instruction, or proselytizing. H.R. 7

---

[123] *See, e.g.*, Lemon v. Kurtzman, supra (fact that most of the teachers in the Catholic schools were nuns and rest were largely lay Catholics found to support finding that schools were "an integral part of the religious mission of the Catholic church"); Hunt v. McNair, 413 U.S. 734 (1973) (fact that religiously affiliated college had no religious qualifications for faculty weighed in determining whether state could issue bonds to subsidize the construction of academic buildings); Committee for Public Education v. Nyquist, 413 U.S. 756 (1973) (imposition of religious restrictions on faculty appointments found to be one element in rendering sectarian elementary and secondary schools constitutionally ineligible for state maintenance and repair grants); and Roemer v. Maryland Board of Public Works, 426 U.S. 736 (1976) (finding that religiously affiliated colleges did not make hiring decisions "on a religious basis" relied on in part in upholding direct public grants to colleges).

[124] Indeed, in some decisions the Court has given that factor no weight at all. *See, e.g.*, Bradfield v. Roberts, 175 U.S. 291 (1899) (upholding construction of wing at a hospital run by an order of Catholic nuns on the condition the wing be used for the medical care of the poor) and Tilton v. Richardson, 403 U.S. 672, 681 (1971) (in finding several religiously affiliated colleges not to be so permeated by religion as to be ineligible for federal construction grants for academic buildings, the Court placed primary emphasis on the fact that the schools "were characterized by an atmosphere of academic freedom rather than religious indoctrination").

further buttresses this prohibition by requiring that any religious activity be entirely separate from the publicly funded program and that any participation in such activity be wholly voluntary. But the underlying assumption of charitable choice has been that religious organizations ought to be able to retain their religious character and employ their religious faiths in carrying out the subsidized programs. That, it is said, is what makes their programs distinctive and, in some cases, more effective. Thus, given this assumption and the various possibilities for how particular subsidized programs might be implemented, it seems likely that constitutional questions will inevitably arise in the implementation of direct aid programs under charitable choice, notwithstanding its prohibitions on the use of direct aid for religious worship, instruction, and proselytization.

In addition, it should be noted that *Mitchell* involved an in-kind aid program – educational supplies and equipment. All of the Justices in *Mitchell* expressed doubt that direct grants of **money** to religious entities could pass constitutional muster even under the Court's loosened standards for direct aid programs; and direct grants of money are what seem contemplated in the programs to which charitable choice now applies or would have been applied under the House-passed version of H.R. 7. Justice O'Connor, joined by Justice Breyer, stated in *Mitchell* both that "[t]his Court has recognized special Establishment Clause dangers where the government makes direct money payments to sectarian institutions" and that a direct subsidy "would be impermissible under the Establishment Clause."[125] Justice Souter, joined by Justices Stevens and Ginsburg, stated:

> [W]e have long held government aid invalid when circumstances would allow its diversion to religious education. The risk of diversion is obviously high when aid in the form of government funds makes its way into the coffers of religious organizations, and so from the start we have understood the Constitution to bar outright money grants of aid to religion.[126]

Justice Thomas, joined by Chief Justice Rehnquist and Justices Scalia and Kennedy, asserted that neutrality is the essential constitutional criterion governing public aid programs that benefit religious entities. But he, nonetheless, observed that "we have seen 'special Establishment Clause dangers' ... when *money* is given to religious schools or entities directly

---

[125] Mitchell v. Helms, *supra*, at 843 (quoting Rosenberger v. Rector and Visitors of University of Virginia, 515 U.S. 819, 842 (1995) and 841, respectively (O'Connor, J., concurring in the judgment).

[126] *Id.* at 890 (Souter, J., dissenting).

rather than, as in *Witters* and *Mueller*, indirectly."[127] These statements are all *dicta* and do not indicate with any certainty how the Court might rule on a case involving a particular grant or cooperative agreement. But they do indicate constitutional doubt about direct money grants.

In addition, it deserves notice that one federal district court, in a decision handed down some years prior to *Mitchell*, held religious discrimination in employment by a religious organization in a position **specifically** funded by a government grant to be unconstitutional.[128] Neither *Agostini* nor *Mitchell* addressed the constitutionality of direct monetary subsidies. On the other hand, it should also be noted that, although not in direct conflict, a federal appellate court recently upheld a state program providing general aid to colleges, including religiously affiliated ones, as applied to a Seventh Day Adventist college, notwithstanding that the college "gave an express preference in hiring ... to members of the Church."[129] Another recent case that was thought to raise the question of the constitutionality of public funding of an agency that discriminated on religious grounds in its employment practices turned out not to do so. In *Pedreira v. Kentucky Baptist Homes for Children, Inc.*[130] the federal district court held that the firing of an employee because of her lesbian lifestyle by an organization whose Christian values abhorred homosexuality did not involve religious discrimination, because the organization's policy did not require employees to accept or practice its religious beliefs but only to conform to a behavioral requirement.

As a final observation, it also deserves notice that formal neutrality as the controlling constitutional principle did gain the adherence of four Justices in *Mitchell v. Helms, supra* (Chief Justice Rehnquist and Justices Scalia, Kennedy, and Thomas). This perspective contends that the critical constitutional elements governing direct public aid to religious entities are whether the aid itself is secular and whether it has been distributed in a religiously neutral fashion, *i.e.*, without preference for religious entities. From this perspective it makes no difference whether the institutional entity eventually uses the aid for religious purposes or not. A slight shift in the

---

[127] *Id.* at 818-19, quoting *Rosenberger, supra*, at 842 (Thomas, J., plurality opinion) (emphasis in original).

[128] Dodge v. Salvation Army, 48 Empl.Prac.Dec. 38619, 1989 U.S.Dist.LEXIS 4797, 1989 WL 53857 (S.D. Miss. 1989) (establishment clause held to bar the Salvation Army from firing a Wiccan from her position as Victims Assistance Coordinator in a Domestic Violence Shelter, both of which were substantially funded by public grants, on the grounds that public funding of such discrimination would have a primary effect of advancing religion and would entangle the government in the religious purpose of the Salvation Army).

[129] Columbia Union College v. Oliver, 254 F.3d 496 (4th Cir. 2001).

[130] 186 F.Supp.2d 757, 86 FEP Cases 417 (W.D. Ky. 2001).

membership of the Court, thus, could foreshadow further changes in the Court's jurisprudence in this area.

(10) WHAT COURT SUITS INVOLVING CHARITABLE CHOICE OR SIMILAR PROGRAMS HAVE BEEN FILED OR DECIDED SO FAR?

At least seven pertinent suits have been initiated, four of which have been decided (at least in part). In *Freedom from Religion Foundation v. McCallum*[131] a federal district court on January 7, 2002, struck down as unconstitutional the public funding of a Wisconsin welfare-to-work program operated by an organization named Faith Works which employed a "faith-enhanced" version of the Alcoholics Anonymous 12-step program as a central element of its residential recovery services to male drug and alcohol addicts. The program was funded by $600,000 in direct grants from the governor's discretionary fund under the federally funded welfare-to-work program. Using the *Lemon-Agostini-Mitchell* test described above, the court found that the grants served a secular purpose, did not define their recipients on the basis of religion, and did not precipitate excessive entanglement. But it held that the grants resulted in religious indoctrination attributable to the government. It described Faith Works as a holistic program that sought to "indoctrinate[] its participants in religion" and concluded that "religion is so integral to the Faith Works program that it is not possible to isolate it from the program as a whole." Safeguards in federal and state law barring the use of funds for religious purposes, it asserted, "exist only on paper" and are "insufficient to insure that public funding ... does not contribute to a religious end." Although the state welfare-to-work program was funded under the federal welfare reform statute and thus was subject to the charitable choice provisions of that statute, the court found the suit not to challenge the constitutionality of charitable choice on the grounds that charitable choice itself bars the "direct funding of religious activities." This decision is being appealed.

The plaintiffs in *McCallum* also challenged the constitutionality of a public subsidy given Faith Works by the Wisconsin Department of Corrections to provide its residential addiction recovery services to designated offenders. In handing down the decision described in the previous

---

[131] 179 F.Supp.2d 950 (W.D. Wis. 2002).

paragraph, the trial court reserved decision on this issue pending further fact-finding. But on July 26, 2002, the court held this program to be constitutional.[132] In contrast to the foregoing program, the Department of Corrections did not make an outright grant to Faith Works but reimbursed Faith Works for the cost of services rendered to each offender who chose to participate. Agents for the Department recommended treatment programs to offenders which included Faith Works and a number of other halfway houses in the Milwaukee area; and the agents could order the offenders to go to a specific secular treatment program. But the Department's regulations stressed that participation in Faith Works had to be wholly voluntary; and thus agents were required to inform offenders of the religious nature of the program, to make clear that the offender did not have to go there, and to offer an alternative secular program. The court found that the agents complied with the regulations scrupulously. Consequently, although finding it to be a "close question," the trial court held that "offenders participate in Faith Works as a result of genuinely independent, private choice and that this choice makes the Department of Corrections contract with Faith Works an indirect program that does not covey a message of endorsement."

As noted in the preceding section, *Pedreira v. Kentucky Baptist Homes for Children*[133] did not involve a federally funded program but raised the question of whether the establishment clause allows the direct public funding of a religious entity that fired an employee who was found to be a lesbian on the grounds her sexual orientation violated the agency's religious beliefs. In this instance the religious entity received substantial state funding for its services to children. On July 23, 2001, a federal district court held that the employee's dismissal did not constitute religious discrimination, because her lifestyle was not premised on any religious beliefs and Baptist Homes did not require her to accept its religious beliefs. It only required conformity, the court said, with a behavioral requirement. The court held over for trial, however, a separate claim alleging that public funds were being used by Baptist Homes for the purpose of religious indoctrination in violation of the establishment clause. In so doing it rejected an argument that *Mitchell* dictated judgment for Baptist Homes, saying that "*Mitchell* is factually dissimilar from this case," in part because this case involves "direct monetary assistance." Thus, the case continues to have implications for charitable choice.

---

[132] Freedom from Religion Foundation, Inc. v. McCallum, 214 F.Supp.2d 905 (W.D. Wis. 2002).
[133] *See* n. 116.

A third suit, *American Jewish Congress v. Bost*[134] contended that a welfare-to-work training program funded under the TANF program in Brenham, Texas, was permeated with the teachings of Protestant evangelical Christianity and even used public funds to purchase Bibles for participants. The suit contended that the funding had been provided pursuant to directives promulgated by then-Governor George Bush that implemented the provisions of charitable choice. But the case was dismissed as moot because the program was no longer being funded by the state. On May 15, 2002, however, the U.S. Court of Appeals for the Fifth Circuit remanded the case to the district court for decision on the constitutional issue and the possible award of monetary damages.

In *ACLU of Louisiana v. Foster*[135] a federal district court enjoined Louisiana from disbursing any more funds in its abstinence education program to organizations or individuals who used the funds to convey religious messages or that were pervasively sectarian. The court found that a number of the grantees in the program were using the public funds to purchase religious materials and to engage in specifically religious activities and that in some of the organizations "religion is so pervasive that a substantial portion of their functions are subsumed in the religious mission." Although finding the purpose of the program to be secular, the court held the funding of the pervasively sectarian institutions and of programs that conveyed religious message or otherwise advanced religion to violate the establishment clause.

American Jewish Congress v. Bernick charges that the California Employment Development Department gave an unconstitutional preference for religion by inviting only religious groups to submit proposals on how to use $5 million in job training funds under TANF. The suit charges as well that the bid invitation violates the mandate of charitable choice that religious and non-religious providers be given equal treatment. The suit is pending in the California Superior Court for the County of San Francisco.

A suit similar to *Pedreira* has recently been filed in Georgia challenging the constitutionality of religious discrimination against employees and applicants for employment by a Methodist children's home that receives substantial funding from the state. In *Bellmore v. United Methodist Children's Home and Department of Human Resources of Georgia*, a youth counselor who was fired when it was found she is lesbian and a psychotherapist who was denied employment because he is Jewish, along

---

[134] ___ F.Supp.2d ___ (W.D. Tex. 2000), *aff'd in part*, 37 F.Appx 91, 2002 U.S.App.LEXIS 10091 (5th Cir. 2002).
[135] 2002 U.S.Dist. LEXIS 13778 (E. D. La. 2002).

with several taxpayers, have sued the Methodist Children's Home on the grounds that the establishment clause forbids an entity receiving public funds from discriminating on religious grounds in its employment practices. Georgia contracts with the home to provide foster care and counseling services, and the Home reportedly receives about 40 percent of its budget from the state. The case is pending in the Superior Court of Fulton County, Georgia.

Finally, on October 3, 2002, the American Jewish Congress reportedly filed suit against the Federal Corporation for National and Community Service charging that its AmeriCorps program has unconstitutionally subsidized religious instruction in sectarian schools. The suit alleges that the program has supported teachers in sectarian schools who provide instruction in religion and has provided grants to entities such as the Alliance for Catholic Education which incorporate prayer and worship activities into their daily activities. The suit is pending in the United States District Court for the District of Columbia.

APPENDIX: COMPARISON OF CHARITABLE CHOICE STATUTES WITH TITLE II OF H.R. 7, AS ADOPTED BY THE HOUSE, AND EXECUTIVE ORDER 13279

	1. States purpose to be to allow FBOs to participate on same basis as secular organizations without impairing their religious character or religious freedom of beneficiaries	2. Bars gov. from discriminating on the basis of an FBO's religious character	3. Requires that FBOs remain independent of government and retain control over expression of religious beliefs	4. Bars gov. interference with FBOs' form of internal governance or displays of religious symbols	5. Provides that Title VII exemption allowing FBOs to discriminate on religious grounds in their employment practices is not affected by receipt of public funds under designated programs
Welfare Reform (42 USCA 604a)	X	X	X	X	X
Community Services Block Grant (42 USCA 9920)		X	X	X	X
Children's Health Act (42 USCA 300x-65)	X	X	X	X	X (also allows FBOs to require adherence to rules forbidding the use of drugs or alcohol)
Community Renewal Tax Relief Act of 2000 (42 USCA 290kk)	X	X	X	X	X (also states that this does not affect the applicability of any other employment non discrimination statute)

	1. States purpose to be to allow FBOs to participate on same basis as secular organizations without impairing their religious character or religious freedom of beneficiaries	2. Bars gov. from discriminating on the basis of an FBO's religious character	3. Requires that FBOs remain independent of government and retain control over expression of religious beliefs	4. Bars gov. interference with FBOs' form of internal governance or displays of religious symbols	5. Provides that Title VII exemption allowing FBOs to discriminate on religious grounds in their employment practices is not affected by receipt of public funds under designated programs
Title H of H.R. 7, the "Charitable Choice Act of 2001"	X (also to provide aid in most effective manner and to broaden the Nation's social services capacity)	X	X	X (also bars gov. from requiring changes in religious terms in charter documents or in name)	X (also states that Title VII exemption and charitable choice override contrary provisions in program statutes, and specifies that Title VII continues to apply)
Executive Order 13279 (Dec. 16, 2002)	X	X	X	X (is silent on internal governance but also allows FBOs to retain religious terms in charter documents and in name and to choose board members on a religious basis)	Amends Executive Order 11246 to provide that religious organizations entering into procurement contracts with the federal government can discriminate on religious grounds in their employment practices but is silent on Title VII

	6. Bars discrimination against beneficiaries on basis of religion or a religious belief	7. Requires gov. to provide those who object to FBO's religious character an accessible alternate provider of equal value	8. Requires gov. to give notice to beneficiaries of right to an alternate provider	9. Requires programs to be consistent with the establishment clause	10. Requires programs to be consistent with the free exercise clause	11. Bars use of direct aid for sectarian worship, instruction, or proselytization
Welfare Reform (42 USCA604a)	X (also on the basis of a "refusal to actively participate in a religious practice")	X		X		X
Community Services Block Grant (42 USCA 9920)				X		X
Children's Health Act (42 USCA 300x-65)	X (also on the bases of a "refusal to hold a religious belief or a refusal to actively participate in a religious practice")	X	X	X		X
Community Renewal Tax Relief Act of 2000 (42 USCA 290kk)	X	X	X (imposes duty on "program participants" as well, and requires them to "ensure" individual makes contact with alternate provider)	X	X	X

Title H of H. R. 7, the "Charitable Choice Act of 2001"	X (also on the basis of "a refusal to hold a religious belief," and requires for direct aid programs that participation in religious activities be voluntary)	X (alternative must be "unobjectionable to the individual on religious grounds")		X (also requires that religious activities be separate from subsidized activities)
Executive Order 13279 (Dec. 16, 2002)	X (also on the basis of "a refusal to hold a religious belief, or ... to actively part. in a religious practice," and requires that part. in rel. activities be voluntary)		X	X (also requires that religious activities be separate in time or location from subsidized activities)

	12. Requires FBOs to certify compliance with # 11	13. Requires FBOs to be subject to same accounting requirements as non-FBOs for use of funds	14. Allows audits of FBOs but requires public funds be segregated from FBOs' own funds	15. States that public aid to FBOs is aid to the individual or family and not to religion or the organization's religious beliefs or practices	16. States that public funding is not to be deemed a government endorsement of religion or of an FBO's religious beliefs or practices	17. States that Title VI, Title IX, Section 504, and Age Discrimination Act remain applicable to FBOs receiving assistance or providing services
Welfare Reform (42 USCA 604a)		X	X (allows, but does not require, funds to be segregated)			
Community Services Block Grant (42 USCA 9920)		X	X			X (bars discrimination on the basis of race, color, national origin, and sex, and states that Age Discrimination Act, Section 504, and Title II of the ADA are applicable)
Children's Health Act (42 USCA 300x-65)		X	X			
Community Renewal Tax Relief Act of 2000 (42 USCA 290kk)		X	X			
Title H of H. R. 7, the "Charitable Choice Act of 2001"	X (also with the voluntariness requirement of # 6)	X	X (requires segregation for direct aid, allows it for indirect aid, and mandates an annual self-audit)	X (specifies that Title VI still applies to direct aid programs)	X	X
Executive Order 13279 (Dec. 16, 2002)						

	18. States that intermediate grantor has same duties as gov. in making subgrants but, if an FBO, retains all rights of FBOs	19. Allows suits for injunctive relief in state or federal court for alleged violations	20. Provides that charitable choice will apply to state funds that are commingled with federal funds	21. Requires states to accept training of drug counselors by FBOs that is "equivalent" to usual educational requirements	22. Allows Depts. to "voucherize" all covered social services programs where "feasible and efficient"	23. Authorizes training and technical assistance program for "small non governmental organizations"
Welfare Reform (42 USCA 604a)		X				
Community Services Block Grant (42 USCA 9920)	X (refers only to duties)					
Children's Health Act (42 USCA 300x-65)	X	X	X			
Community Renewal Tax Relief Act of 2000 (42 USCA 290kk)		X (only against federal government in federal court)		X		
Title H of H.R. 7, the "Charitable Choice Act of 2001"	X	X	X		X	X
Executive Order 13279 (Dec. 16, 2002)						

INDEX

A

accountability standards, 23
accountability, 2, 4, 8, 22-26, 29
Age Discrimination in Employment Act, 69
Agency for International Development, 35, 47
American Federation of State, County and Municipal Employees (AFSCME), 28
American Jewish Committee, 19
American Jewish Congress, 89
Americans with Disabilities Act, 69, 70

B

Baptist Joint Committee on Public Affairs, 29, 30
Baptist, 29, 30, 71-73, 83, 86, 88
behavioral requirement, 86, 88
Better Education for Teachers and Students Act, 63
Bibles, 89
Breyer, Justice, 81, 85
Bush, Governor George, 89
Bush, President George W., 1, 3
Bush, President, vii, 30, 34, 36-39, 43-46, 60, 63

C

CARE Act of 2002, 36, 54, 60, 61
Catholic Charities USA, 41
Catholic Relief Services, 3
Center for Public Justice, 6, 7, 17, 20, 24, 29
Charitable Choice Act of 2001, 1, 4
charitable choice law, 2
charitable choice legislation, 2, 14, 16-18, 23, 35, 36, 46
charitable choice policies, 1
charitable choice provision, 3, 63
charitable choice statutes, 33, 34, 38, 39, 40, 44, 49, 63, 65, 66, 68, 70, 72, 74-76, 83
charitable giving, 4, 34, 36, 54, 55, 59-61
Charity Aid, Recovery, and Empowerment Act of 2002 (CARE bill), 2, 4, 8, 11, 14, 16, 20, 24-26, 29
child abuse, 4
Child Care and Development Block Grant, 41
Christian, 7, 9, 16, 71, 72, 83, 86
church congregations, 3

Civil Rights Act, 16, 39, 50, 57, 65, 67, 69
Community Action Agencies (CAAs), 27
Community Development Block Grant program (CDBG), 11, 51
Community Renewal Tax Relief Act of 2000, 16, 43
Community Services Block Grant, 10, 42, 49
community services, 9, 28
Community Solutions Act of 2001, 20, 21, 36, 45, 53, 54
community-based organizations, 2, 6, 8, 11, 13-15, 20, 27, 46
Compassion Capital Fund, 45, 46, 60, 61
competitive relationships, 27
crime prevention, 4, 9, 11

D

Department of Agriculture, 5, 35, 47
Department of Education, 36

Department of Health and Human Services (HHS/DHHS), 35, 38, 46, 49
Department of Housing and Urban Development, 10, 35, 50
Departments of Labor and Heath and Human Services, 15
direct aid programs, 42, 85, 94
direct funding programs, 42
domestic agenda, 1, 3, 43
domestic violence, 11, 47, 64
Drug Abuse Education, Prevention, and Treatment Act of 2001, 62

E

economic depression, 9
elderly services, 4

Elementary and Secondary Education Act, 63, 80
Emergency Shelter Grant program, 51
employment discrimination, 57, 67, 73, 83, 84
employment nondiscrimination, 69, 72, 73
employment practices, vii, 34, 36, 37, 39, 48-52, 54, 56, 58, 61, 64, 67-72, 76, 83, 84, 86, 90
employment requirement, 50
equal treatment provisions, 4
establishment clause, 24, 58, 65, 75-81, 83, 85, 86, 88-90, 93
evaluative data, 2, 10, 13

F

Faith Works, 87
faith-based initiative, 1-5, 7, 8, 14, 17, 18, 22, 28, 30, 34, 35, 38, 46
faith-based legislation, 4
faith-based organizations (FBOs), vii, 1-30, 35, 39, 45, 49, 52, 57, 91, 92, 95, 96
faith-based social service programs/organizations, vii, 37, 52
FBO-delivered programs, 8, 13, 14
Federal Emergency Management Agency (FEMA), 52
federal financial assistance, 47, 48
federal funds, 1, 3-5, 13, 16, 18, 19, 21, 23, 25-28, 30, 39, 40, 57, 64, 66, 68, 69, 74, 75, 96
federal government's housing, 33
federally assisted services, 4, 30
federally funded program, 69, 88
federally funded services, 2, 3, 11, 19, 26, 57, 64
federally funded social services programs, 33
First Amendment, 38, 40, 41, 57, 73, 75, 76

Index

G

gay, 57, 71, 83
General Accounting Office (GAO), 14
Ginsburg, Justice, 85

H

Habitat for Humanity, 41
HIV/AIDS, 9
HOME Investment Partnerships program, 51
Homeland Security Act, 4
Homeless Educators Linking Providers and Services (HELPS), 14
homeless programs, 3
Hope for Homeownership of Single-Family Homes, 51
House Rules Committee, 58
Housing Opportunities for Persons with AIDS, 51
housing, 4, 5, 9-11, 35, 47, 50, 64
hunger, 4, 64

I

Indianapolis Front Porch Alliance, 8

J

Jewish, 19, 41, 71, 89, 90
job training, 4, 5, 47, 89
juvenile delinquency, 4, 47, 64
juvenile justice, 11, 64
Kennedy, Justice, 85
Kennedy, Justice, 86

L

Legislative Analysis, 10, 13, 16, 17, 20, 23, 25, 26, 29
Lemon-Agostini-Mitchell test, 87

lesbian, 57, 71, 83, 86, 88, 89
long-term services, 10, 11, 12
Lutheran Services in America, 41

M

maximum feasible participation, 27
Methodist, 73, 89
Metropolitan Housing and Community Development Corporation (MHCDC), 9
ministerial exception, 73
monetary damages, 89
money, 10, 29, 85

N

National Association of Counties (NACO), 22
National Association of Social Workers (NASW), 14, 17
national networks, 3
No Child Left Behind Act of 2001, 63
nongovernmental organizations, 11, 12, 23, 24, 60, 66
nongovernmental provider, 2, 3
nonprofit organizations, 15, 22, 27, 52

O

O'Connor, Justice, 81, 85
Office of Faith-Based and Community Initiatives, 3, 10, 13, 30, 35, 43, 44, 49, 51
Older Americans Act (OAA), 11, 64

P

Pedreira v. Kentucky Baptist Homes for Children, 86, 88

Personal Responsibility and Work Opportunity Reconciliation Act of 1996, 16, 49
policy options, 10, 13, 16, 17, 20, 23, 25, 26
prayer, 90
pregnant, 57, 71, 72
Projects for Assistance in Transition, 49
Protestant evangelical Christianity, 89
Protestant, 71
public aid programs, 79, 85
public attention, 1, 3, 4, 7
public funding, 7, 14, 38, 41, 51, 56, 72, 86-88
public funds, 22, 34, 38, 39, 50-52, 55, 56, 66, 67, 70, 72, 75, 76, 83, 88-91
Public Health Service(s) Act, 43, 50, 74
publicly funded programs, 38, 76

R

REDC, 9, 10, 22
Rehnquist, Chief Justice, 85, 86
religious activities, 17, 19, 22, 25, 26, 44, 48, 49, 52, 58, 65, 71, 77, 79, 87, 89, 94
religious beliefs, 30, 48, 64, 74, 76, 77, 86, 88, 91, 95
religious denominations, 10
religious discrimination in employment, 59, 70, 84, 86
religious discrimination, 40, 58, 59, 68, 70, 75, 84, 86, 88, 89
religious education, 10, 85
religious entities, 33, 42, 51, 70, 71, 77, 81, 83, 85, 86
Religious Freedom Restoration Act, 50
religious freedom, 2, 3, 38, 43, 63, 91
Religious Freedom, 39

religious indoctrination, 42, 77, 79, 81, 84, 87, 88
religious instruction, 26, 48, 90
religious observance, 17
religious organization(s), vii, 2, 3, 23, 33-43, 49, 50, 52, 54-58, 60, 63-68, 70-76, 78, 85, 86
religious school, 52
religiously affiliated colleges, 42, 84
religiously sponsored organizations, 41
Rural Economic Development Center (REDC), 9, 10, 22, 23

S

Salvation Army, 41, 59, 72, 73, 86
Scalia, Justice, 85
Scalia, Justice, 86
Seattle Hebrew Academy (SHA), 52
Second Chance Homes, 37, 62
sectarian elementary and secondary schools, 42, 79, 80, 84
sectarian schools, 80, 90
sectarian worship, 18, 40, 93
secular alternatives, 2, 10, 19, 20
separation of church and state, 58
Seventh Day Adventist college, 86
Seventh Day Adventist, 83, 86
Shelter Plus Care, 51
social service organizations, 35, 46, 52, 57
social service programs, 11, 13, 19, 46, 48, 49
Social Services Block Grant program, 61
social services programs, 33-36, 38, 41-44, 47, 48, 51, 56, 60, 63, 75, 84, 96
social services providers, 41, 60, 70
Souter, Justice, 85
state and local governments, vii, 2, 4, 8, 12, 14-16, 19-23, 26-29, 47
Stevens, Justice, 85

Substance Abuse and Mental Health Services Administration (SAMHSA), 49, 50
substance abuse prevention and treatment, 49
substance abuse programs, 3, 62, 74
substance abuse, 3-5, 10, 43, 47, 62, 69, 74
supportive housing, 51
Supreme Court, 42, 56, 71, 72, 76, 77

T

tax incentives, 1, 3, 4, 33, 36, 54, 55, 59, 60
taxpayer, 13, 57
Temporary Assistance for Needy Families (TANF), 3, 10, 16, 37, 42, 43, 49, 76, 89
The Aspen Institute, 3, 10, 12
The Bush Administration, 13
The White House, 35, 52, 59
Thomas, Justice, 81, 85
Thomas, Justice, 86

U

U.S. Agency for International Development, 5
U.S. Conference of Mayors, 8

United Jewish Communities, 41
unmarried, 57, 71, 72

V

voluntary religious activities, 17, 19
voucher system of payment, 24

W

welfare-to-work, 9, 42, 87, 89
White House Office for Faith-Based and Community Initiatives, 36
workforce development programs, 6
workforce development, 6, 10
Workforce Investment Act (WIA), 11, 64
working relationships, 2, 27
World Vision Inc., 3
worship activities, 90

Y

Youthbuild, 51